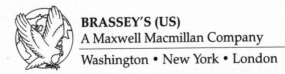

PROTECT YOURSELF, YOUR FAMILY, YOUR HOME

Checklists Against Crime

James B. Motley

with

Lois M. Baron

BRASSEY'S (US)
A Maxwell Macmillan Company

Washington • New York • London

Brassey's (US)

Editorial Offices
Brassey's (US)
8000 Westpark Drive
First Floor
McLean, Virginia 22102

Order Department
Brassey's Book Orders
c/o Macmillan Publishing Co.
100 Front Street, Box 500
Riverside, New Jersey 08075

Brassey's (US) is a Maxwell Macmillan Company. Brassey's books are available at special discounts for bulk purchases for sales promotions, premiums, fundraising, or educational use through the Special Sales Director, Macmillan Publishing Company, 866 Third Avenue, New York, New York 10022.

Library of Congress Cataloging-in-Publication Data

Motley, James B.
    Protect yourself, your family, your home: checklists against crime / James B. Motley, with Lois M. Baron.
        p.   cm.
    Includes index.
    ISBN 0-02-881074-0
    1. Crime prevention. 2. Burglary protection. 3. Violence—Prevention.
HV7431.M685   1993
362.88—dc20
                                                                    93-31314
                                                                    CIP

10 9 8 7 6 5 4 3 2 1
Printed in the United States of America

CONTENTS

INTRODUCTION

There are good reasons to worry about crime. According to the Federal Bureau of Investigation's (FBI) *Crime in the United States, 1991*, an average of one violent crime—murder, rape, robbery, or aggravated assault—takes place every seventeen seconds. And property is stolen about every two seconds. Given these statistics, you should worry enough about crime so that you're motivated both to prevent it and to take actions that protect yourself, your family, your property, and your neighborhood. However, you should not become so concerned about it that your fears inhibit the way you live. It's one thing to avoid visiting bad neighborhoods at night; it's another never to go out at night at all.

Informed judgment can help you modify your actions without unreasonably limiting what you do. For example, if a woman wants to go out alone at night to visit a friend, she can. She just needs to take reasonable precautions and pay attention to what's going on around her. She calls her friend right before she leaves to tell the friend what time to expect her, so the friend can both put on the porch light and be ready to greet her at the door. When she leaves the house, she makes sure her doors and windows are locked. She checks as she heads to her car, which she has left locked, to see if anyone is nearby. She has her car key ready in her hand. Her car is well serviced and has plenty of gas. She drives in the center lane on well-lighted streets. After she parks in a well-lighted spot, she takes a look around before she opens her car door to see who else might be there. She locks her car when she gets out. Her friend greets her at the door, and they spend an enjoyable evening together. This woman is alert and prudent. She is not frozen by fear.

This scenario *is* a bit simplistic. Depending on the neighborhoods, the car, and the house involved, much more can be done—car and house alarms can be set, or the woman might choose to carry an alarm or chemical spray with her, for example. Also, if the woman has to ride public transportation, she must take even more precautions. Our point in offering this example is this: Many ways to keep yourself safe are simple and free. Taking preventive measures does not mean you are paranoid; it simply means you're careful. Some anxiety helps you play it safe, which is good. But too much means that you are letting criminals dictate how you live your life. You need to find a balance.

Crimes happen constantly across the nation—an average of one every two seconds, measured by the FBI's crime index. Your own particular risk is affected by your age, race, income, education, and where you live. Everyone should take precautions. And depending on their situation, some people should take more.

In this book, we define common crimes and outline pertinent facts. We use the FBI's annual report, *Crime in the United States, 1991*, and the Bureau of Justice Statistics' publication *Criminal Victimization in the United States, 1991*, to determine who is most at risk. Then, through checklists, we outline how to lessen your risk.

With *Protect Yourself, Your Family, Your Home*, our intent is to help you make informed decisions about your safety. We want you to do everything possible to prevent crime, and we feel that, if you take these actions, you will gain the confidence to live, work, and travel safely. Remember, criminals are less likely to victimize confident people.

Our information has been gleaned from many sources. Despite a rising crime rate, much of the information has stood tried and true for years, for most of personal and property security is common sense. It makes sense to lock your doors when you leave the house for any reason. Yet, one out of five burglars didn't have to force his way into the house he burglarized. It just makes sense to lock your car door. Yet thousands of cars have been stolen from people who left their car doors unlocked *and* their keys in the ignition!

There is no guarantee that you will be safe just by following the advice given in this book. Some people will do everything to avoid being victimized and still suffer from crime. Others will do nothing "right" and never be accosted or robbed. But if you make it a habit to use the suggestions found here, you will cut your risk of being robbed, stolen from, and attacked. Just remember the themes of this book: Pay attention and use common sense. Avoid becoming a victim. If your preventive efforts don't work, you must have an alternative plan. It could save your life.

PROTECT YOURSELF, YOUR FAMILY, YOUR HOME

Checklists Against Crime

1

AT HOME:

Inside and Outside

HOUSES

After the first burglary, Charlie F. had the police do a home security check, but he made only one of many changes they suggested. Even after the second robbery, he didn't cut back his shrubs, didn't change his locks, and didn't always lock his doors and windows. Two robberies later, he shook his head in disgust. "There's nothing left to steal," he said.

Burglary is *the unlawful entry of a structure to commit a felony or theft*. Two out of every three burglaries in 1991 were of residences. And, as in Charlie's case, 20 percent of the time the burglar did not have to force his way into the home.

People have a notion that homes are burglarized at night, but the truth is, burglaries and attempted burglaries are evenly divided between day and night. With the advent of the two-income household, more and more homes stand empty during the day. Burglars like that.

In 1991 the greatest number of burglaries took place in July and August; February had the fewest burglaries. Nationwide, the burglary rate is 1,252 per 100,000. Southern states have the highest rate per 100,000: 1,498; followed by the West (1,324), the Midwest (1,037), and the Northeast (1,010).

Burglary victims suffered overall losses estimated at $3.9 billion in 1991. The average home lost $1,281 worth of goods per burglary.

Who does the dirty work? Adults accounted for 81 percent of those arrested for burglary. The FBI reports that juveniles were caught for burglary at a rate of approximately 18 percent in cities, 20 percent in rural counties, 23 percent in suburban counties, and 25 percent in towns with fewer than 10,000 residents.

The most important thing you can do to prevent a burglary is to make it look as if someone is home. Burglars, whether they're operating at night or during the day, do not want to encounter anyone while they steal.

No home is burglarproof. Given enough time and the right equipment, a burglar can make his way into any building, including fortresses and museums. In an ordinary home, if a burglar really wants in, he can break or cut open a window. Most burglars, though, are opportunists looking for an easy target, such as Charlie's.

The single biggest attraction to a burglar is concealment. If he can work on a door or window without being detected, he will. Doors are the easiest way into a home for anyone, including intruders. In more than 90 percent of residential burglaries, the thief enters the home through a door or window. About a third of the time, the burglar comes through a window, which is usually not locked in the first place.

A secured home is much less attractive than one that isn't. Although nothing is 100 percent fail-safe, a few security measures go a long way in keeping you and your possessions safe.

If you choose to install an alarm system in your home, you need to understand its limitations and requirements, including what it demands of *you*. An alarm requires attention. If you're not willing to be conscientious about using it, you're better off spending your money in other ways.

There are perimeter alarms, motion-sensitive alarms, and heat-sensitive alarms. When choosing an alarm system you need to take into consideration your home, what you need to protect, your budget, who lives in the home, and how elaborate and sensitive a system you want to deal with. You don't want your small children and pets constantly setting off your system, for example. You should read all the literature you can before choosing a particular system and get at least three estimates before you select an installer. Besides being a good business practice, this will keep you from being swindled by a phony company.

When installing a system, homeowners often choose to put the system in on the first floor, because they figure that's where the greater risk is. With expensive systems, installation on one floor also holds down costs. If you choose to do this, you'll need to make sure that burglars can't get to your other floors and, if they do, that it will be difficult for them to get in. A gang of burglars had great success in the early part of 1993 in a high-class neighborhood outside Washington, D.C., by going into homes through second stories. A couple of times they took a ladder from a neighboring yard to use. Another time they climbed a trellis to the second story and lowered valuable items with a rope made of the victim's silk ties. As this example illustrates, you can't rely solely on an alarm system to protect your belongings.

Given the rising crime rates and violence they see reported day after day, many people wonder if they should get guns to protect their homes. The short answer is no. People with guns are much more likely to injure or kill a family member or friend with guns than to use them to defend themselves against an intruder. Hundreds of people are killed each year when a gun is discovered by a curious child, grabbed by an enraged spouse, or used by someone who doesn't clearly see his target.

If you choose to keep a gun, store the ammunition separate from the weapon. Buy a lock for the trigger. Be certain that you'll have the will to use deadly force against someone. If you hesitate, your assailant can take your gun away and use it against you.

Finally, make sure you can see the person's face before you pull the trigger.

Dogs can make a great deterrent. But they also need a lot of care. Furthermore, a watchdog merely alerts you to danger; guard dogs are supposed to attack intruders. Guard dogs, however, don't make good family pets. You must constantly attend to them to make sure they don't attack every stranger, such as family friends they haven't met yet and other "intruders."

The bottom line is, if you don't want a dog, don't get one just because you think it will protect you and your home. Instead, you might do better buying dog accoutrements, that is, a dog house and a heavy chain to attach to it. Or you could paint a properly vicious-sounding name on a big dog bowl to put on your back step or just inside sliding glass doors. Scruff up a chew toy and leave it lying around in a visible spot. A burglar who sees these objects will wonder where the dog is—and sometimes the question is as effective as seeing a dog itself.

The first order of business in securing your home is to strengthen the structure itself. Next you should make sure your actions around your home keep you safe. Remember, the best lock is worthless if you fail to use it. By securing the entries to your home and making safe practices into habits, you can discourage burglars who are looking for the home of least resistance.

Preventive Measures

Door Locks

❑ Always lock your doors and windows, even if you're just running outside to see what is causing a commotion.

❑ When you move to a new home or apartment, have a licensed locksmith change all the locks on the home. It is also a good idea to change your locks periodically.

☐ Burglars like entrances that are out of sight, so give extra protection to your basement door, such as a hardened-steel padlock.

☐ Make sure all the doors leading outdoors—and the one from your garage to your house—are at least 1 3/4 inches thick and solid.

☐ Make sure the door frames to outside doors are sturdy and well constructed.

☐ Replace the spring-bolt latch on doors leading outside and the one from your garage to your house with a dead-bolt lock that has a throw (the part that fits into the door frame) of at least 1 inch. An inch and a half is better. Secure the strike plate (the part that attaches to the door frame) with 3-inch screws. These must be long enough to penetrate the doorjamb and the underlying framing stud.

☐ Use L-shaped strike plates.

☐ Consider using a double-cylinder lock if your door has a window in it or if the door is within three feet of any kind of glass window or sliding door. A double-cylinder lock requires you to use a key from the inside as well as the outside to open the door. Such a lock prevents a burglar from knocking out a windowpane, reaching inside, and unlocking your door. Be sure to keep the key close enough to find in case of fire but far enough away from the door that a burglar couldn't reach in and get the key.

☐ Install a lock collar—a metal ring that fits around the outside lock cylinder. It prevents housebreakers from yanking the whole lock cylinder out.

☐ Put a hardened steel insert inside your lock to prevent the bolt from being sawed off.

❏ Investigate the different locks available. They include electronically controlled ones, ones with a counter to tell you how many times a lock has been opened and closed, and locks whose tumblers can be rekeyed at will.

❏ Consider using more than one lock on your door. Space the locks 12 to 18 inches apart to dissipate the force of a kick aimed at either one.

❏ Consider getting a lock with a vertical (rather than horizontal) deadbolt. These are stronger.

❏ Secure a chain lock into solid wood with screws at least 2 inches long so that someone cannot use his shoulder to pull the lock off the door frame. The links in the chain should be heavy and welded. The chain itself should be short enough that the door cannot be opened more than an inch or two.

❏ Use a chain guard that consists of a welded-steel, brass-plated loop of chain mounted on the door next to the doorknob with 2-inch screws. The loop slips over the doorknob and lets the door open to only a slit.

❏ Replace worn locks. If your key can slip out when it is only halfway turned, you may leave the core half turned, but you did not lock it that way. Anyone can open it by continuing the turn with a paper clip. Your lock is also faulty if the cylinder turns without the key being fully inserted.

❏ Install antipry plates to protect the bolt from being popped out of the opening it fits into.

Doors

❏ Install a peephole in your outside doors.

❏ Replace removable hinge pins with a hidden or nonremovable type on all doors that open out.

☐ Protect your door from being taken off its hinges by doing the following: Take out two screws opposite each other from both leaves of each hinge. Insert a long screw or concrete nail into the jamb leaf, letting it stick out about half an inch. Drill out the opposing screw hole in your door. Do this in the top and bottom hinge of the door. When you close the door, someone can remove the hinge pins, but the protruding screws will hold the door firmly in place.

☐ Strengthen secondary doors once you have exterior doors in good shape.

☐ Replace wooden cellar doors with steel hatch doors bolted into concrete. Then bar the doors from the inside.

Sliding Glass Doors

☐ Make sure it is installed properly, so the movable panel opens and closes on the interior, not the exterior, side of the fixed-glass panel.

☐ Place a stick the length of the panel in the track of the sliding door to prevent someone from sliding the door open.

☐ Drill a downward-sloping hole through the top channel into the top part of the door frame. Then put in a quarter-inch pin or heavy nail through the frame and into the door. When you leave the house for extended periods, use this security measure along with other locks on your sliding doors.

Garage Doors

☐ Always lock your garage door, especially if the garage is attached to your home.

☐ Install an automatic garage-door opener that opens the door and turns on a light. If you see a burglar, drive away immediately and call the police.

❑ To make your garage-door opener more secure, get an outside key-lock switch. Wire it to your opener with bell wire so that by simply turning the key, the door will open. Then get rid of the radio receiver. This can prevent accidental openings of your door, which can occur when radio-operated openers are set off by a passing auto transmitter or airplane.

Other Doors

❑ Put a flap over your mail slot with a tight spring that will keep it closed. Add a strong, bottomless, steel basket covering the inside of the slot. The basket keeps a would-be intruder's wires and tools away from locks. It also makes your mail drop out of sight rather than letting it fly out at an angle where a snooper can see it.

❑ Protect *all* entrances to your home, including crawl spaces, skylights, roof accesses, and vents.

Windows

❑ Keep your windows locked as much as you can.

❑ Replace the windowpanes in exterior doors with laminated glass, if your neighborhood and security needs warrant the expense. Experts suggest you use a .600-inch polyvinyl-butryal (PVB) interlayer laminated glass.

❑ Make sure your window latches work properly.

❑ Pin double-hung windows. Drill a quarter-inch hole through the inside window frame and into the outside frame on each side of the window. Insert a nail or metal pin into the hole, leaving a quarter inch out so that it can be removed easily from the inside. This prevents someone from removing one frame and entering your home.

☐ Attach window air-conditioning units with long screws or bolts fitted into the window and structure. If a burglar takes out the window unit, it gives him a big opening into your home.

☐ Get a lock for sliding windows that clamps onto the upper or lower rail and locks the window closed or only partially open.

☐ Use accordion window gates securely anchored to a solid window frame.

☐ Consider using security bars on your windows. They do have drawbacks: they are expensive, are often ugly, and unless they have a release mechanism, may trap you inside in the event of a fire.

☐ Get rid of louvered windows. A thief can easily slip these windows out of their grooves using a thin screwdriver or piece of metal. If you want to keep them, install protective bars on the outside or glue the slats into place with epoxy.

☐ Replace your glass windows with a strong, wireless safety glass or high-strength plastic glazing.

☐ Cover basement windows with a wire-mesh grate. Use No. 8 or No. 10 steel wire welded into a half-inch round frame, and install it with burglarproof hinges and closing fasteners from a local ironworks. Or install security bars. If you need to use the windows as a fire escape, buy bars that you can collapse easily from the inside. Be sure to install the mesh grate or the bars from the inside.

☐ Add shutters on the outside or inside of your windows. Hang them on pivot hinges attached to the house wall or window frame. Shut them with a sturdy inside latch; a flat steel bar across the inside on retainer brackets adds even more security.

❏ Clear the way between the street (or to neighbors) and street-level and basement windows that are out of public view. Remove or prune shrubs that obscure windows.

❏ If you don't need a window for ventilation or for escape during a fire, fasten it closed permanently.

❏ Install large picture windows or similar expanses of glass in rabbetted jambs with the frame's solid wood or metal facing outward so no one can tamper with the glazing compound.

Outside Your Home

❏ Protect the alley side of homes with chain-link fence. In really high-risk areas, barbed wire across the top of the fence does an even better job of securing your property.

❏ Plant hedges of thorny plants, such as holly or roses, to discourage unwelcome guests.

❏ Trim your bushes so you don't provide cover for an intruder.

❏ Light the outside of your home at night.

❏ If you can afford one, install an auxiliary, battery-powered lighting system.

❏ Keep all walkways, paths, and steps well lit.

❏ Post your house number clearly on your front door. Keep an outside light on so that the number is visible from the street to help police find your home if they need to respond to an emergency call. If your home abuts an alley, also post your number on your back door or fence.

❏ Leave your porch light on when you're home as well as when you go out for the evening. Otherwise you set up a pattern that clearly tells a burglar whether you're home.

☐ Don't advertise your single status on your mailbox. Don't use your first name or Ms. or Miss (or Mrs. with only a first name).

☐ Cut back lower tree limbs that are close to upper windows, porches, or roofs leading to upper windows.

☐ Remove any trellises that someone could clamber up to enter your home from the second story.

☐ Keep ladders secured and out of sight. Don't leave ladders up if you're doing yard work and need to run to the hardware store.

☐ If your home abuts an alley, coat your drainpipes with anti-climb paint to prevent anyone from climbing them to your roof or second-story windows.

Inside Your Home

☐ Consider installing an alarm system in your home. Keep in mind that sensitive alarms can be set off by the rumble of trucks along the street if you live in a thin-walled building. Infrared, photoelectric eye, and perimeter systems are better in a noisy setting.

☐ Consider getting a remote, wireless lighting control center. The control module goes in your bedroom, and you plug lights and appliances such as the TV or radio into remote modules; you replace switches for outdoor lights with two-way remote selective units. Using this system lets you turn on any lights or appliances you wish by punching the appropriate button. Some models have built-in timers. If you hear a suspicious noise, you can flip the switch and probably frighten any housebreaker away.

☐ If you don't opt for a lighting control center, put some lamps and perhaps your TV on timers.

☐ Try a bedroom-door alarm that goes off if someone touches the doorknob. It awakens you with a persistent, piercing sound.

☐ At night, leave some lights on throughout the house and make precautionary checks throughout the evening.

☐ Use a photosensitive timer on your porch or front-door light.

☐ Install a bolt on your bedroom door, and use it when you go to bed.

☐ Put an identifying mark on your valuables. Burglars are less likely to take property that can be identified as stolen because it will be harder for them to sell. Etching tools are often available on loan from police departments. You can choose to use invisible ink, which is visible when illuminated with ultraviolet light. This would obviously be more useful in identifying your property if it was recovered by the police than in acting as a deterrent. Also, inventory your possessions so that you'll be able to make an accurate report to both the police and your insurance company if anything does get stolen.

☐ If you have utility meters in your home, check with your utility companies to see if they'll read your gas, electric, and water meters annually. Better yet, have these meters relocated outside so you don't have to admit strangers.

☐ Keep valuables out of sight. Particularly keep them away from windows, where passersby might be tempted to smash the glass, grab an object, and run.

☐ Have a two-line phone so that if an intruder takes the phone of the hook, you can still call for help on another phone.

☐ Put away small expensive items, credit cards, cash, purses, and wallets that could tempt visitors.

☐ Keep all stock certificates in a safe-deposit box or at your broker's.

☐ Don't leave checks lying around, either filled out or blank. They can be taken and cashed.

☐ Don't point out or discuss your valuables to strangers such as delivery men, service men, and door-to-door sales personnel.

☐ Report to the proper authorities any streetlights that burn out in your neighborhood.

☐ Get a free security check courtesy of your local police, if they offer it.

☐ If you have had lots of trouble, consider making a tape of a barking dog. Play it on a continuous-play tape recorder loud enough to be heard outside the house.

At the Door

☐ Never open the door without first seeing who is on the other side.

☐ Never let a stranger in or let him get you out of the house. For anyone who comes to the door asking to use the phone for emergency assistance, your best strategy is to keep the door shut and offer to place the call for them to summon the police or an ambulance.

☐ If you are a woman, call out "I'll get it, Ralph" (or some other male name) near the door before taking the usual precautions and opening the door. Let the visitor think you are not alone.

☐ If a repair or delivery person comes to the door, you can start the shower so he thinks someone else is home; ask a friend to be on hand; leave the front door open and stand by it until he leaves; or keep a friend on the phone until he leaves.

☐ Slide a rubber doorstop under the door as you open it a crack to check a stranger's credentials. If the person tries to shove the door open, the doorstop will slow him down while you get help or run out the back door.

☐ Close your door immediately when you enter your home. If you place a small table right by the entrance, you can deposit your packages there, close the door, and then put your parcels away. Too many burglars and rapists have come in through that open door while the victim is in another part of the house.

When You Go Out

☐ Ring the doorbell or knock when you come to what is supposed to be an empty house. This gives any intruder time to clear out; odds are a burglar doesn't want a confrontation either.

☐ Don't leave messages on the door.

☐ If you don't have an answering machine, turn the ringer on your phone off—or to its lowest setting and pile a few blankets on top—so that a prowler casing your home won't hear your phone go unanswered and think the coast is clear.

☐ Arrange for someone to house-sit while you attend family events such as weddings, bar mitzvahs, and funerals that have been mentioned in the newspaper. Some criminals scan the papers for such notices and then pay a visit while you are out.

Last But Not Least

☐ Never put your name or address on your key ring. If you lose your keys, you don't want someone else helping himself to your belongings.

☐ Install an intercom set.

☐ Don't hide door keys in obvious places, such as under the doormat or in the mailbox.

☐ Keep emergency phone numbers by your bedroom phone.

☐ Ask your neighbors to help keep an eye on your house—and promise to do the same for them.

☐ Exchange house keys with your neighbor and explain to each other how your security system works.

If Burglars Strike While You're Home

☐ If the alarm goes off during the night, immediately call the police.

☐ Yell for your companion to get the gun while you call the police, even if you don't have a companion or a gun.

☐ If you come home to find a strange van or other vehicle at your place, drive off and find a phone to call the police.

☐ If you come home and a door or window is open or broken, don't go in. Find a phone and call the police.

If Your Home Has Been Burglarized

☐ Call the police. Note all the details of your conversation, including your case number.

☐ Leave everything exactly as you found it until the police have completed their work.

☐ If your home has been vandalized and items thrown on the floor, take photographs.

☐ Notify your insurance company. Submit a list of stolen items. If you discover later that other items have also been taken, make an addition to your list promptly.

☐ If credit cards, automatic teller machine (ATM) cards, or checks were taken, notify the financial institutions that issued them.

☐ Determine how the thief entered and see what you can do to prevent a second visit.

☐ If there is no sign of a forced entry and you're certain you didn't leave the doors unlocked, have a locksmith change the cylinders.

Making your home look occupied is probably the single most effective action you can take to prevent burglaries. But you also should take the other measures outlined above to deter especially daring burglars, rapists, and other intruders.

APARTMENTS

In some apartment buildings, a doorman is on duty twenty-four hours a day, and restricted access to the building becomes effective around 11:00 P.M. In others, access is controlled by a key to the front door. Despite these and other measures, apartment tenants continue to be victims of crime.

Your apartment may merely have the illusion of security. Such homes were the site of 23.7 percent of violent crimes in 1991 when the crime involved a stranger (39.6 percent for rapes by strangers, 47.2 for robberies by strangers, and 17.5 percent for assault by strangers). A number of tenants have sued apartment management for lapses in security that resulted in the tenant being assaulted or sexually attacked.

As with houses, the typical burglar selects apartments that offer quick and quiet entrances and exits. Your job is to make the burglar want to go elsewhere to commit his crimes. You can do that by making sure the building is as secure as possible, by "hardening" your own apartment, and by acting safely. In other words, you want to change your apartment physically to make it as difficult to enter as possible. And then make sure you don't compromise the safety of your home, for example, by leaving windows unlocked while you're gone for the weekend.

An apartment does have at least one advantage over a detached single-family home: it usually has fewer doors and windows that need to be secured.

In addition to making sure that you have done all you can to secure your living accommodations, you should encourage management to beef up security measures—by installing more lighting, putting in security cameras, and so forth. You should also encourage your neighbors to work together to make your building more secure and start a neighborhood watch program.

Preventive Measures

Door and Window Locks

☐ Keep your doors and windows locked.

☐ Make sure the front door of your apartment has a dead-bolt lock and a peephole or other viewer to look at callers before you open the door.

☐ Install a front door that is solid wood—or metal sheathed—with a dead-bolt lock. Doors should be at least 1 3/4 inches thick.

☐ If you have a sliding glass door, make sure it is installed properly, that is, so the movable panel opens and closes on the interior, not the exterior, side of the fixed-glass part.

☐ Determine which doors and windows could conceivably serve as an entry for intruders so that you can take measures to secure them. Balcony doors and windows that could be entered from any direction—from a neighbor's window, neighbor's balcony, or the roof—all need to be protected.

☐ To protect sliding glass doors and windows from being lifted out of their tracks, drill small holes in the top of the trough, then insert screws, tightening them just enough that the door or window skims the surface of the screw heads.

☐ Take extra precautions with windows leading to fire escapes. Use a locked metal gate even when the window is open.

☐ Have the locks changed when you move in.

☐ Make sure all windows have good locks.

☐ If you live on the first floor, install window bars.

☐ Do not sleep with your windows open.

☐ Nail the transom above your door shut if you don't need it for light or ventilation. It may not be big enough to crawl through, but a burglar may be able to reach down through it and unlock your door. If it is glass, block the opening with a solid panel nailed into the door frame. If you need it for air or light, put in steel bars across the hole.

Inside Your Apartment

☐ Close the blinds and draperies at night. Stay away from the windows when you're undressing.

☐ Have a solid bedroom door that self-locks and that has a dead-bolt lock.

☐ Install dead-bolt locks on your inside doors as well, or at least on your bedroom as a second line of defense.

☐ Use rubber doorstops to keep anyone from pushing the door farther open than you want him to.

☐ Keep a telephone in your bedroom. Ideally you should have two lines on your phone so that if an intruder takes the phone off the hook in the living area, you can still call for help behind the safety of your bedroom door.

☐ Keep emergency phone numbers by your bedroom phone.

☐ Always make it appear as if someone is home. Use timers to turn on lights, a radio, or the TV.

☐ Always verify a stranger's identity before you open the door.

☐ If you are alone and not expecting anyone, if someone knocks, talk as if you were having a conversation with someone else in the apartment before you open the door.

☐ Offer to make a call for anyone who comes to your door asking to use the phone to summon emergency assistance. Do not let him or her in.

☐ Don't let people you don't know or deliveries you aren't expecting enter the building.

☐ If you have valuables such as paintings or a coin collection, consider installing an alarm system.

Outside Your Apartment

☐ Check with the local police department (try the crime prevention unit, if there is one) to see if you have any rights as a tenant to change locks and make any other changes to strengthen security.

❏ Determine how the landlord controls the master key or duplicate keys. Insist that management not keep a duplicate key to your apartment. If that doesn't work, put the duplicate key in an envelope, tape it shut, and write your name across the flap. Tell the superintendent to let you know when and why he uses your key. This should make him think twice about using it indiscriminately.

❏ In a building with security, don't let a stranger in with you when you enter the building. Politely tell people waiting to enter the building that they must be let in by the party they came to see.

❏ Insist that management keep bushes and other obstacles to your line of sight around windows and entrances trimmed back.

❏ Your parking facility should be as close to your apartment as possible and well lighted.

❏ If your building has a garage in the basement, as you drive in, be alert to those who may try to sneak into the garage before the automatic door closes. If someone does, inform the doorman, guard, superintendent, or police immediately.

❏ Ensure that your apartment grounds do not have large trees, shrubbery, or other landscaping features that could provide hiding places for burglars.

❏ Make sure the entrances, stairwells, and hallways are well lighted. Insist that your landlord replace blown lightbulbs.

❏ Make a pact with your neighbors that if anyone sees a flier stuck on or under another's door, you'll push it all the way inside. Burglars pretending to pass out advertising or religious material can stick fliers halfway under every door and return several hours later to see which ones haven't been picked up. Odds are, those are the apartments that will get burglarized.

☐ Always lock your doors and windows when you go out, even if it's to run out to see what is causing a commotion. Burglars have been known to pull the fire alarm in an apartment building and then check for unlocked doors after the building is evacuated.

☐ If you are a woman, put only your last name on your mailbox.

☐ Do not tell your fellow tenants any personal information you do not want repeated to someone else.

☐ If you see or hear something suspicious, call the landlord, front desk, or the police.

☐ Insist that laundry, storage, and trash areas in the apartment complex be made available only to tenants.

☐ Do not go to the laundry room alone.

☐ Use the laundry room only during the day.

☐ Set your air conditioner to "circulate" rather than turning it off when you are gone during hot summer months; an idle air conditioner is a dead giveaway that no one's home. Putting it on circulate saves energy but makes as much noise as when the air conditioner is set to "cool."

☐ If you hear a noise that might be a burglar in another part of the house, make a lot of noise, and yell, "George, I think I hear a burglar." If you wake up to a burglar in your room, pretend to keep sleeping. The last thing you want to do is confront an intruder who may panic and assault you.

☐ Try to vary your routine so that people who might have access to your apartment won't know the best time to find it empty.

Elevators

☐ Be cautious about getting into elevators with people you do not recognize as apartment tenants.

☐ Be wary of getting into an elevator with one or more men if you are the only woman.

☐ Stand back from the elevator door while you wait for its arrival. You don't want to be in a position where you can easily be pulled or shoved into the elevator.

☐ If you are in an elevator and someone suspicious gets on, get out and wait for the next elevator.

☐ In an elevator, stand next to the control panel and be ready to hit the alarm button and the buttons to all the floors. You want to make noise and be able to get off the elevator as soon as possible if something happens. Do not hit the stop button. You do not want to be trapped.

☐ Do not ride in an elevator if the roof escape hatch is ajar.

☐ When you get off the elevator, look all the way around so that no one can come from behind and surprise you as you walk down the corridor.

When Coming Home

☐ Be cautious as you enter your lobby. If a stranger or unsavory-looking person is there, decide whether you should notify your neighbors or security. If in doubt, take a walk around the block and see if the person is still there when you get back. If so and you can't get help from neighbors or security, call the police.

☐ If your mailbox is in a low-traffic area or out of sight of the lobby, be cautious when approaching it.

☐ Treat corridors as you would streets. Look around and be alert.

☐ When you get off the elevator, look all the way around so that no one can come from behind and surprise you as you walk down the corridor.

☐ When you get to your apartment door, you want to get inside quickly, but you shouldn't concentrate so hard on opening the locks that you don't pay attention to anyone coming toward you.

☐ Don't pause to read any fliers posted to your door. You can pull off fliers to read later. Pick up your mail or newspapers, and go immediately into your apartment.

☐ When opening your apartment door, you should stand sideways so that you can observe what's going on in the corridor.

☐ Always lock the door right after you enter your apartment.

If Your Apartment Is Burglarized

☐ Report it to your insurance company.

☐ Report it to the police.

☐ Report it to building management.

☐ Alert your neighbors.

Remember, home security must be used to be effective. Lock those doors and windows!

(See AT HOME: HOUSE.)

CAMPUSES

Enter to learn—but while you're there, make sure you don't learn the hard way about being the victim of a crime.

Campuses, whether they're part of a city or their own microcosms, are as likely to be the setting of a crime as anyplace else. There's nothing sacred about those hallowed halls of learning. In fact, you should stay out of those halls if they're deserted after dark!

In recent years more attention has been given to making campuses safe from rapists and thieves, but no one should assume that any campus is trouble-free. Before attending a college, you should ask to see the statistics of crime on campus. You need to know how troubled the area is.

Many college administrations have implemented security systems across campus, such as security phones, that make it easier for students to get help. Other actions include adding lights across campus, more security patrols, and escort services home from the library.

Preventive Measures

❑ Always lock your doors and windows at night in your dorm room.

❑ Draw the curtains or blinds.

❑ Lock your dorm room whenever you leave it, even if it's just to go down the hall.

❑ Don't prop open dorm doors or allow strangers into the building.

❑ Avoid deserted places, including cutting through empty buildings late at night.

❑ If you study in the library, stay in rooms with five or six people in them, so you don't have to find another room if a couple of people leave.

☐ If there are community bathrooms, use one that has a lock on the inside.

☐ Never go to the laundry room late at night.

☐ Tell your roommate where you are going and when you expect to return.

☐ Women, never walk alone at night. If your college doesn't have an escort service, contact the administration to organize one.

☐ Women, make sure you know all the measures a campus administration has taken to protect you against rape and what resources are available to you.

If Anything Happens

☐ Call campus security.

☐ Call the local police.

☐ Notify your resident adviser or dorm supervisor.

Learn how to be safe on a campus.

(See AT HOME: APARTMENT, HOUSE; STREET CRIME: RAPE; VEHICLE THEFT.)

TELEPHONES

A burglar may use the telephone to find out whether your home is vacant, or someone may use it to harass you. In either case, you can take several precautionary measures in your dealings on the telephone.

Also make certain you and your family members know how to use the phone in an emergency. It could save your lives.

Preventive Measures

☐ Women should list initials, rather than their first names, in the telephone directory.

☐ Never tell a stranger who calls when you'll be out. It may sound like an innocent telemarketer, but you never know for sure.

☐ Don't give your phone number to a caller. Ask instead what number he was calling, tell him, "You have the wrong number," and hang up. In fact, give out as little information over the phone as you can to strangers.

☐ Never let a stranger know you're alone. If someone asks for your spouse, instead of responding, "He's not here," say, "He can't come to the phone right now; may I take a name and number?"

☐ Instruct your children never to let a caller know they're alone.

☐ Tell your baby-sitter exactly what you'd like the sitter to say to callers when you're out. Rather than saying that you're out for the evening, the sitter should say, "Mr. and Mrs. Blake are very busy right now; may I take a message?"

☐ Ideally you should have two lines coming into your bedroom in case an intruder takes the phone downstairs off the hook. Or use a cellular phone in your room. It will work if the intruder has cut the line(s).

☐ Make sure the message on your answering machine doesn't give away too much information either, such as when you expect to be back home.

☐ If a caller claims to be a police officer, request that the officer visit you in person so you can check his credentials. Or ask if you can call the person back, and use the phone directory to verify the number.

When Harassed

☐ Hang up immediately on obscene phone callers.

☐ Report all obscene calls to the police, giving the date and time of the calls. If the calls continue, the police and phone company can act to trap the caller.

☐ If the calls are threatening as well as obscene, call the FBI.

☐ Look into the services the phone company offers to deter harassing calls, such as Caller ID, call trace, and call block.

☐ If necessary, change your telephone number.

☐ If you get repeated obscene phone calls, tap on the mouthpiece with a pencil or pen and say, "Operator, this is the pervert who has been calling me; you can trace the call now." Then stay on the line a minute before hanging up to simulate an actual tracing.

☐ Consider using a voice-disguising device. Such a device can make a woman sound like a man or a child like an adult to ward off strangers looking for a vulnerable target.

Emergencies

☐ Always carry change for a phone call with you when you're away from home. And make sure change for a call is hidden in each member of your family's clothing, too.

☐ Teach your children to dial 0 for an operator to help them get the police, the fire department, or an ambulance; teach older children about 911. Rehearse procedures with them. They should know how to give their name, location, problem, and phone number. They should also know their parents' work numbers.

❏ Post emergency telephone numbers on each telephone in your home.

The telephone can be extremely useful, but sometimes burglars and rapists use it for their benefit. By being aware of this potential danger, you're one step ahead.

2

AT WORK

Most people would not consider the post office as a hazardous place to work. Yet twice in 1993 disgruntled employees burst into postal offices and opened fire, killing and wounding colleagues and supervisors. According to the U.S. Department of Justice, 12 percent of all violent crimes and 20 percent of all thefts happen at work. And 7.9 percent of rapes occur in commercial buildings.

You spend a great portion of your day at work. You need to take precautions to keep yourself and your possessions safe. Building security plays a part in how safe you are at work, but your security depends largely on your own actions. The first half of this chapter focuses on staying safe as an employee. The second part deals with the concerns of a business owner or manager.

EMPLOYEE CONCERNS

Preventive Measures

☐ Ideally, you should avoid work that takes you into high-crime areas.

❏ Your parking facility should be as close to your work site as possible and well lighted.

❏ Lock your car when you leave it.

❏ Make sure the entrances, stairwells, and hallways in your office building are well lighted. Insist that the building manager replace blown lightbulbs and add more lighting if necessary.

❏ Be most alert and cautious before and after regular hours. Lock your door if you're working late alone or in the company of other employees you don't know well. Keep the phone number of building security taped to your telephone. If your building doesn't have guards at the main entrance, make sure that door is also locked if you can. Never prop it open for anyone.

❏ Use the bathroom during regular business hours. In the morning wait till coworkers arrive or, after hours, use it before everyone leaves for the day.

❏ If you work early or late, let someone—a supervisor, the building superintendent, or the elevator operator—know you're there.

❏ Avoid confrontations with fellow employees. Let a third party settle any dispute.

❏ Don't leave your keys or billfold on your desk or in your jacket if you're not wearing it.

❏ Put your purse in a desk drawer, and lock it.

❏ When leaving your office, put calculators, radios, and other small valuables in a desk drawer and lock it.

❏ Avoid using stairwells by yourself. Don't enter stairwells to avoid attackers.

- [ ] Ask strangers in the halls if you can help them if you're accustomed to knowing everyone there.

- [ ] Report any unrequested "repairman" removing your office equipment; check with the office manager to see if this person is supposed to be taking the material.

- [ ] There's generally safety in numbers—when heading to your car, getting into an elevator, or walking in stairwells. If you're a woman, ask someone you trust to walk you to your car after dark.

- [ ] Look in the backseat before you get into your car.

Elevators

- [ ] Be cautious about getting into elevators with one man or, if you are the only woman, a group of men who look suspicious.

- [ ] Stand back from the elevator door while you wait for its arrival. You don't want to be in a position where you can easily be pulled or shoved in.

- [ ] If you are in an elevator and someone who makes you nervous gets on, get out and wait for the next elevator.

- [ ] In an elevator, stand next to the control panel with your back to a wall and be ready to hit the alarm button and the buttons to all the floors. You want to make noise and be able to get off the elevator as soon as possible if something happens. Do not hit the stop button. You do not want to be trapped.

- [ ] Do not ride in an elevator if the roof escape hatch is ajar.

- [ ] Pay attention to which way the elevator is going before you get on it. It is better to wait than to go to the basement or the roof.

If Anything Happens

☐ If you are assaulted in any way or if you have belongings stolen, report the incident to your supervisor, building security, and the police.

☐ Ask that your coworkers be alerted so that they can take extra precautions.

Stay safe at work. Be alert, take basic precautions, and use common sense.

EMPLOYER CONCERNS

Every company needs to keep its assets safe from theft and vandalism. It has been estimated that 15 percent of all business failures in a given year could be directly attributed to employee dishonesty. Obviously, employers should make their employees aware that dishonesty, great or small, can put them on the unemployment rolls in more ways than one.

Statistics show that half of the nation's workers steal from their employers. About 16 percent do so in significant quantity and either use the supplies themselves or give them to friends and relatives. About 5 percent resell stolen items for profit.

Losses from larceny of all types—computer fraud, bad checks, shoplifting, and everything else—adds as much as 15 percent to the cost of goods and services.

A business owner can lose money and material in three ways: from an outside thief, from employee theft, and from inadequate or violated procedures. Employees should be instructed in how to protect the company's information as well as its material assets. Careless revelations can inadvertently open the way for burglaries at employees' homes, industrial espionage, and litigation.

Just as you protect your business property from theft, you need to take measures that protect your employees from assault and theft. Often security measures do both.

The security that a business should put in place varies according to the nature of the business. A manufacturing plant has different worries about theft than a downtown law office has, for example. What we present here is an overview of the kinds of actions and devices that can be used to secure your business. First you should assess the threats: Computer theft instead of shoplifting? Industrial espionage or employee theft? Then seek out experts on that subject, such as your local police force or the Small Business Administration (SBA). The police can do a security check for your business, and the SBA publishes a variety of information on deterring different sorts of business crime.

Preventive Measures

General Security

☐ Make sure the outside world has a clear view into your store. Thieves aren't crazy about the "fishbowl" effect.

☐ Use cash controllers.

☐ Make sure your doors and windows are sturdy and have good locks.

☐ Always lock your doors and windows after hours.

☐ Put in a good alarm system. If your system is faulty and is always giving false alarms, the police are likely to give it a lower priority.

☐ Keep any side or back doors you have locked (but do establish an escape route in case of fire). Install a pressure-sensitive floor mat to announce intruders.

☐ Secure any openings that might be large enough for a burglar to squeeze through, including air shafts.

☐ Join with your business neighbors to hire a night watchman. Make sure the watchman has specific instructions and duties so that he's busy, alert, and supervised.

☐ Ensure that the outside of your building is well lighted, including the roof if it's vulnerable.

☐ Bolt down equipment and furniture where feasible.

Robbery

☐ If someone holds you up, don't resist. Nothing is as valuable as your life.

☐ Stay as calm as possible. Don't make sudden moves, and speak in a low, calm voice.

☐ If a robber seems uncertain about what to do after you've given him the money, suggest that you lie down on the floor "like the last robber had me do while he left."

Shoplifting

☐ Prosecute shoplifters. If you don't, word will get around. Then you'll be hit more often than places that do go to the trouble—and it is inconvenient and time consuming—to prosecute shoplifters.

☐ Set up a bonus plan for employees who help spot and apprehend shoplifters.

☐ Look out for people with darting eye movements. They may be people checking to see if anyone is watching before they steal merchandise.

☐ Rearrange your stock so that the most frequently stolen merchandise is the least accessible.

☐ Have cashiers check to make sure small merchandise is not hidden away inside larger items.

☐ Have cashiers look for any merchandise a customer may simply be holding as the clerk rings up other items. The customer may be absentminded, or he may be intending to stroll out of the store with the unpaid-for items.

☐ Have customers check their shopping bags or backpacks at the counter as they enter your shop.

☐ Keep an eye on any package or clothing item that could be used as a receptacle for shoplifted goods. This includes sports jackets, handbags, diaper bags, the hood of a sweat-shirt, and brassieres.

☐ Insist that a customer may make only one monetary trans-action at a time. If someone wants change and then wants different denominations, it's easy for a clerk to get confused and give the customer too much money.

☐ Mandate that a manager approves all exchanges and refunds. Then you can avoid having a clerk get confused by an aggressive customer trying to exchange merchandise for more expensive goods without paying the difference or to get a refund on an item he never paid for in the first place.

☐ Control the merchandise that is taken into and out of fitting rooms in some way.

☐ Train your employees to be observant. For example, a cus-tomer should not go into the dressing room wearing one blouse and leave wearing another.

☐ Your staff should watch people closely after they've taken merchandise to make sure no switch is made with an accomplice.

☐ Use tamper-proof price labels, bar codes, or tags on plastic strings to prevent customers from switching price tags.

☐ Avoid showing a customer too many small items at once. If the clerk's attention is diverted, it's too easy for the cus-tomer to pocket some of the goods.

- [ ] Put small expensive items in locked display cases.
- [ ] Watch shoppers' hands.
- [ ] Make sure the pickup department hands merchandise over only to customers who have proper receipts.
- [ ] Make sure shoppers have a receipt for any item you gift-wrap for them.
- [ ] Consider the layout of your store. Does it offer thieves protection from detection?
- [ ] Block off unused checkout aisles.
- [ ] Keep mannequins and displays where employees can keep an eye on them.
- [ ] Make sure the clerk doesn't have to turn his back on the customer to ring up a sale.
- [ ] Put credit card receipts out of sight immediately so no one can copy down someone else's credit card number.
- [ ] Put the registers in full view of doorways to guard against people slipping out without paying for merchandise.
- [ ] To ward off shoplifters, keep an eye on loiterers.
- [ ] Install detection devices such as mirrors or cameras in your stock room.

Employee Theft

- [ ] Set a good example.
- [ ] Run a security check on people with whom your firm negotiates major deals.
- [ ] Employ outside firms or consultants to help you spot trouble. Hire a public accountant, an auditing firm, or a shopping service that can help determine if your staff is adequately trained against theft.

☐ Keep track of loans you make to other departments.

☐ Pick up the company mail or have a highly trusted assistant do it. Have that person open the mail and record cash and checks received. This prevents an accounts-receivable clerk from pocketing payments without recording them.

☐ Have people be responsible for different parts of the same job so that they informally check the other's honesty. One person can count inventory while another can record them. The person who opens the mail can keep a tally of receivables to double-check the accounting clerk responsible for entering them.

☐ In the mail room have one person receive mail orders, another pack the boxes, and another run packages through the meter.

☐ Make sure people take their days off. Anyone assuming their duties might detect any embezzling or wrongdoing. Similarly, if you have the backup staff, you can encourage data-processing personnel to take their vacations during the end-of-the-month. That way, someone can check their work during these frantic bookkeeping periods.

☐ Be suspicious of anyone who passes up a promotion so that he or she can stay in a position where valuable information or money is handled.

☐ Set up a security system that will catch thieves from the inside—that is, employees waiting until after closing to walk out with goods.

☐ Control the number of ways your employees can come in and go out. Ideally, everyone should come and go through one door.

☐ Consider forbidding employees from bringing packages into their work areas. That way they won't be able to conceal stolen items in such things as lunch boxes on their way out.

❑ Spot check your trash bins. Employees have been known to dump company property into the trash and then remove it after work.

❑ Engrave business equipment with the company name.

❑ Use a fluorescent powder to mark goods likely to be stolen by employees or to mark cash registers. An ultraviolet light will reveal any wrongdoers.

❑ Set up a policy and a monitored system allowing workers to borrow equipment for home jobs. That way they won't have to steal equipment they need on a short-term basis but can't afford.

❑ Destroy damaged goods instead of letting your employees buy it at a discount. The discount for damaged goods can encourage workers to handle merchandise roughly.

❑ Prevent payroll padding. Make it a policy that anyone added to the payroll must be okayed by you. If you have fewer than fifty employees, sign the checks yourself. Try rotating the payroll disbursement function among the accounting staff.

❑ Forbid employees from punching anyone else's time card.

❑ Keep nepotism to a minimum, and make occasional personnel transfers to break up any cliques that might have turned into a theft ring.

❑ Follow up refunds with a friendly call to the customer to ask if the transaction was handled well. If the customer knows nothing of a refund, it's time to call in the cashier whose initials are on the tape.

❑ Double-check the records of loading-dock clerks. Too many shortages or too many overages may indicate that numbers are being changed. No shortages recorded might point you to an employee who's not counting at all.

- ☐ Get an invoice with all deliveries before a truck is unloaded.

- ☐ Require that goods be counted at the delivery dock and that boxes be opened when your clerk does the counting.

- ☐ Price markers should make their own count of items they tag to see if their count tallies with that from the loading dock.

- ☐ Keep shipping and receiving docks separate, even if you use just a wall or fence. The less confusion there is, the fewer chances there are for thieves to do their work.

- ☐ Lock up stock rooms, marking rooms, and shipping and receiving docks, as well as any other high-priority places in your workplace, when they're not in use.

- ☐ Lock up loading-dock doors.

- ☐ Post a dock guard.

- ☐ Don't give the drivers of your company vehicles the keys to the cargo compartments.

- ☐ Keep control of the keys. Whenever someone with control of one or more keys stops working there, have the locks changed.

Your Office Computers

- ☐ Develop authorization procedures that ensure only authorized users have access to computers.

- ☐ Establish password management protection controls.

- ☐ Program the computer terminal to shut down after a specific time of nonuse and during nonbusiness hours.

- ☐ Develop policies requiring management approval for software changes, and limit those who can make software changes.

☐ Lock or bolt computers to work stations. Lock offices where computers are stored or used.

☐ Lock up computer disks and tapes when not in use.

☐ Secure printouts of passwords and other access information.

☐ Establish contingency plans if notified that information is lost, stolen, or destroyed.

☐ Train new employees in their responsibilities to prevent computer crimes, fraud, and abuse.

☐ Conduct periodic security awareness briefings.

☐ Monitor computer output to see if unauthorized items such as printouts are being produced.

☐ Don't keep automated information in only one place. Back it up.

☐ Know what automated information and equipment requires protection.

Last But Not Least

☐ Empty your registers at the end of the day. Leave the cash drawers open and lighted so potential burglars can see there's no point in breaking into your store.

☐ If someone calls you to say there's an emergency at your store, call the police to meet you there. Otherwise you open yourself up to the possibility of getting robbed by the caller.

☐ Vary your routine so a robber can't tell when cash or valuables are leaving your store.

☐ Watch as someone signs a traveler's check to avoid receiving a stolen or forged one.

☐ Make sure a credit card is current by noting its expiration date; check that the customer's signature matches that on the back of the card; and check the card number against any list of stolen cards the credit card company may have sent you.

☐ Don't cash a personal check that has been taped together.

☐ Look out for forged checks. Watch for smudged checks, misspelled words, and poor spacing of letters or numbers.

☐ Guard against bad checks. Follow company procedures and ask for identification.

☐ Be on the alert for counterfeit money by look and feel. Legitimate tender is printed on special paper available only to the government; it feels more like stiff cloth than paper. On phony money the fine printing of background dots and the filigree work around the border are often darker or filled in.

☐ If you are making a night deposit and the depository door is covered by a sign announcing the machine is out of order and directing you to place your deposit in a nearby "temporary depository," don't do it. You'll never see your money again.

☐ All deliveries and pickups should be made at a reception or shipping area. No messengers or delivery people should be roaming your halls.

☐ Register guests, and issue them an identification (ID) card.

☐ If appropriate, have an interview room for salesmen and other visitors that is just off your reception area.

☐ Search the premises each evening to make sure no one is hiding inside to circumvent your security system.

❑ Contact your police department for periodic security checks.

❑ Contact the Small Business Administration (1441 L St., N.W., Washington, D.C. 20416) for further information on how to prevent business crime.

If Anything Happens

❑ Report it to the police.

❑ If it's a theft, report it to your insurance company.

❑ Prosecute.

The steps you take to protect your business and personnel will depend on the nature of your business. Depending on your business, there are many more security precautions you can take than can be discussed here. Talk to the police, read trade magazines, and seek out experts. Take those steps now!

3

OUT AND ABOUT

A rapist had been working the bike path for several weeks. Word of the attacks had been widely covered in the local media. Yet a policewoman pulling duty as a decoy came across a lone woman jogging at dusk. "Perhaps you shouldn't be jogging alone," suggested the undercover officer. "I refuse to let criminals run my life," retorted the jogger, making it clear that she would continue to run whenever she chose.

You want to be free to go anywhere. And you should be able to. You need to keep in mind, however, that criminals also think they should be able to do whatever they want. And if there's a confrontation because you choose to go where a criminal is prone to be, you're likely to be the loser. Actions have consequences. You need to take those actions that minimize your risk of becoming a crime victim.

Planning is key to your personal security. First, you should plan how to avoid trouble. Then you plan how to handle trouble if you encounter it. You need to consider how to stay safe as you go about your daily routine, running errands, exercising, and relaxing away from home. Think about the risks inherent in the places you travel, shop, exercise, play. Does your regular jogging path take you by a wooded area? Is the parking lot at your favorite grocery store well lighted during the hours you visit it?

Statistics collected by the Bureau of Justice Statistics show that violent crimes—robbery, rape, and assault—take place on a street not near your home 22.7 percent of the time; in a parking lot or garage 10.7 percent of the time; near home 7.1 percent of the time; inside a restaurant, bar, or nightclub 5.6 percent of the time; and on public transportation 1.3 percent of the time.

Here are ways to minimize your risks while you are out and about.

YOUR CAR

Preventive Measures

☐ Always keep your car doors locked.

☐ Before you get in your car, check that the tires are okay, that there are no obstructions in front of the wheels, and that no one has broken into your car.

☐ The ideal is to keep your car windows rolled up or open no more than two inches. If you don't have air conditioning, in the summer your best bet as a driver is to roll the driver's side window all the way down, and the passenger's side window down two inches. Then roll your window back up at stoplights and intersections in rough neighborhoods.

☐ Put any purses or packages in your trunk or under your seat.

☐ Avoid dark side streets at night. Stay on well-lighted and busy thoroughfares.

☐ Don't offer rides to strangers, male or female.

☐ A car phone offers convenience and safety. So does a CB radio, which you can tune to the police channel.

❑ A dummy car phone offers the appearance of being able to call the police if you run into someone who may want to trouble you on the road. If a suspicious car begins to follow you, pick up your dummy receiver and act like you're making a call.

❑ Avoid parking near intersections, stop signs, traffic lights, and bus stops—all favorite locations of muggers and rapists.

❑ If you're a woman driving alone at night, wear a man's jacket and hat. Some fearful people even go so far as to rig up a dummy in the passenger seat to make it look like they're not alone.

❑ Avoid lovers' lanes. They're frequented by muggers and rapists.

❑ Don't stop to help someone on the road who looks like he or she needs assistance. Go to the nearest phone, and call the police or highway patrol.

❑ Avoid idling in neutral. You may need to move away fast.

❑ Never accept a stranger's offer of help if you get in your car and find it won't start. The stranger may have disabled your car. (Keep your window rolled up and door locked.) Instead, if he's persistent in wanting to help, ask him to call a friend of yours, a relative, or the police. If he tries to persuade you to unlock your car, hit the horn and keep hitting it intermittently until he leaves.

❑ If your car won't start late at night in an unfamiliar or bad neighborhood, check to see if anyone suspicious is around. Then get out, lock your car, and go back immediately to the place you just left. If you're on a quiet, dark side street, the best choice is to leave your locked car and return for it in daylight, with company.

❏ If you are pulled over by a police car, confirm that you are dealing with a legitimate police officer. Marked cars have departmental decals on the doors; an officer driving either a marked or unmarked car should have a patch on his sleeve identifying the officer's department and a name tag on the front of his shirt. A legitimate officer will approach you—sometimes on the passenger side of the car for greater safety for the officer—and give his name and his reason for stopping you. Roll the window down only a few inches. If the officer flashes his badge too quickly for you to read, ask to see it again. If you still have doubts, especially regarding the driver of an unmarked car, ask for another piece of identification. If you still can't verify the legitimacy of the officer, ask that an officer in uniform be called.

❏ If you are signaled by an unmarked car to pull over but do not want to do so on a dark or deserted street, indicate to the officer that you recognize the order and intend to comply, and proceed—at a speed no faster than the speed limit—to a police station or well-lighted location. As long as you follow this procedure, you can't be charged with resisting arrest.

❏ If anything bad happens, the best strategy usually is to stay in your car.

If Followed

❏ Do not go home.

❏ If you think someone is following you, do not pull off to the side of the road to see if he passes. He's likely to block your car and commit the crime he had in mind to start with. Instead, turn your car around and see if he does too. Drive to a well-lighted service station or store and spend a little time there, asking for directions or making a purchase. If the car you think is following you has left, get back in your car and drive several streets. If the car reappears, drive back to the well-lighted area and call the police.

☐ Keep to well-traveled, well-lighted areas and try to attract attention. Flash your lights, honk your horn, slow down, and put on your flashers.

☐ Drive to a police station, fire station, or hospital emergency room. Or if one is not close, stop at a service station and call a relative, friend, or police car to escort you home. Or park and lock your car and take a taxi. Tell the taxi driver to wait outside until he sees you're safely inside your destination.

☐ Even if the person gives up the chase, try to get a license plate and report the incident to the police.

☐ If a car following you flashes its lights, do not pull over. If it is a police officer who wants to pull you over, he will use a red or blue flashing light and his siren.

If Your Car Breaks Down

☐ If someone stops to help and you don't want his help, simply say that help is already on its way. If the person lingers, start beeping your horn intermittently. (Don't just lean on your horn; people will assume it's stuck.)

☐ Raise the hood or tie a white rag to the street-side door handle or the antenna. If you were able to pull your car off to the side of the road, stay in the car with your car doors locked. (If you can't get your car off a busy road, you should get out of the car and stand on the shoulder. You risk getting killed if you stay in your car.)

☐ Ask anyone who stops to help to call a friend, relative, or the police for you.

☐ You can tap out the Morse code distress signal with your horn: three short, three long, three short. Signal for two or three minutes, then again only when you think someone might hear you.

(See VEHICLE THEFT.)

PARKING LOTS

Parking lots have space for cars and trucks. They also offer nooks and crannies for rapists, muggers, attackers, and carjackers. According to the Bureau of Justice Statistics, for example, 3.4 percent of rapes occur in parking lots or parking garages. Motor vehicle theft took place in such locations 35.5 percent of the time. To keep you and your car safe, heed the following advice.

Preventive Measures

☐ Choose a parking lot in a busy location.

☐ Park in attended lots if possible.

☐ If you have to leave your key with an attendant, leave only your ignition key.

☐ In a parking garage, try to park close to the attendant, in a well-traveled spot. Avoid dark corners.

☐ Avoid parking spaces next to areas or objects where someone could conceal himself, such as by a Dumpster or a wooded boundary.

☐ If you are parking in a lot during the day but will be returning after dark, park in a space by a streetlight.

☐ Roll your car windows up and lock the doors.

☐ If possible, park on the street edge of the lot, where you don't have to walk through many cars to reach yours when you return.

☐ If you pull into a space next to a car that is occupied, don't get out if something about the person makes you uncomfortable. Find another space.

☐ Before you get out, take a moment to scan the area. Is there normal activity? If there is no one in the lot, it is better to wait a moment to see if someone else parks or if someone comes out of a building. Criminals like to work in isolation; having another person on the scene cuts your chances of being confronted.

☐ When you get out of the car, take another look around to survey the area.

☐ Walk in the open aisles of parking lots, not between cars.

☐ When returning to your car at night, try to pair up with someone who is going in that direction.

☐ To return to your car, walk around the lot, not through it.

☐ Have your car key out before you enter the parking lot.

☐ Going back to your car, walk in the open aisle, but look down the rows of cars as you come to them. When you go down a row toward your car, watch for people loitering or sitting in a car. If it's dark, use a flashlight to look around and underneath your car. If you find trouble, go for assistance from parking lot personnel or the place you just left or from the police, if necessary.

☐ Look under your car to make sure no one is hiding there.

☐ If someone is in your car, run back to the entrance of the lot and shout for help.

☐ If your car looks as if it has been broken into, leave the area and call the police. You don't know where the thief might be.

☐ If your car is disabled—it doesn't start or the tires are slashed—seek help.

☐ Lock your car door immediately after you get into the vehicle.

☐ Keep the windows up until you exit the parking garage.

SHOPPING

Preventive Measures

☐ Shop in locations you're familiar and comfortable with.

☐ Shop with a companion, if possible.

☐ Be wary in public bathrooms. If someone suspicious is in there, leave.

☐ Use the bathrooms in a department store rather than the mall's public bathrooms, which are usually at the end of a long deserted hallway close to delivery bays and exit doors.

☐ If you're visiting several locations on your shopping trip, store your packages in your trunk, and purchase the most expensive items last.

☐ Never put your purse in the shopping cart; keep it on your arm or shoulder.

☐ Check to make sure the clerk hands back your credit card— not someone else's possibly stolen card—after paying for an item. If you do receive someone else's card, tell the manager, not the clerk. The clerk may be the one perpetrating the crime.

☐ If the clerk asks for a phone number, write it down on your check rather than saying it out loud.

☐ Make sure no one is looking over your shoulder while you write out a check; you don't want strangers seeing your address.

☐ Put your credit card and your wallet away before moving away from the cash register.

☐ Avoid self-service places after dark.

☐ If a group of hoods starts following you at a mall, go into a coffee shop until they lose interest.

☐ Avoid passageways that look deserted.

☐ If you're being followed, go into a store and ask for help. Do not go outside and try to get to your car; you're more vulnerable in the open.

☐ Make sure any taxi you take clearly displays the company name and the driver's identification. Make sure the driver is the same person as the one listed on the ID before you get in.

(See OUT AND ABOUT: CREDIT CARD FRAUD; STREET CRIME.)

AUTOMATIC TELLER MACHINES

Preventive Measures

☐ Avoid automatic teller machines (ATMs) after dark.

☐ Try to use ATMs that are secure; that is, either have a guard nearby or require that you use your card to enter the area that contains the teller machine.

☐ Choose a machine in a well-lighted location.

☐ If using a drive-through ATM, use one that is visible from the street.

☐ Drive around the bank once to see if any characters are loitering nearby before you approach the ATM.

☐ Try to take someone with you when you go to use the ATM. It doesn't hurt to have your friend primed to use the CB or the car phone to summon the police.

☐ Stand sideways as you use the machine. Be alert to those around you.

☐ If someone suspicious comes up when you're using an ATM, or you see that you're being watched, leave. Don't complete your transaction. It's better to be inconvenienced than robbed.

☐ Put the money you receive and your statement in your front pocket or purse before walking away. Don't walk away with money in your hands. Count your money in your car with your windows up and your doors locked.

☐ Choose a well-traveled street to use when leaving the ATM. It's safer and easier to determine whether you were followed from the money machine.

CREDIT CARD FRAUD

In 1992, credit card fraud for MasterCard and Visa reached approximately $1 billion industrywide—a substantial increase over the previous year. These losses are eventually passed on to you, the cardholder, in the form of increased costs. Credit cards are simple to use both in the United States and abroad. They provide ready access to cash through banks and ATMs and are often used at restaurants, hotels, and shops. Although convenient, credit cards should be used responsibly. Remember, before charging anything to your credit card that there is no "stop payment" on credit card transactions. Before you sign something irreversible, take time to think about it.

Preventive Measures

☐ Carefully check your monthly credit card statement when you receive it.

☐ Report lost or stolen cards to the issuer immediately. It's a good idea to make a list of your credit cards and the telephone numbers that you should call in case your cards are stolen or lost. Keep the list in a safe place.

☐ Never give your credit card account number over the telephone unless you initiated the call.

☐ Never give your credit card to someone else to use on your behalf.

☐ Never give your account number for any reason other than to make a purchase or to reserve a hotel room or rental car.

☐ Keep your credit card in sight when making transactions. Make sure the store clerk destroys the carbons, doesn't make an extra imprint, and returns your card before you leave the store. Verify that the clerk returned your card, not somebody else's card, prior to leaving the counter.

☐ Before you sign the credit card voucher, compare the imprinted and handwritten charges.

☐ Destroy carbons, and keep old credit card slips and statements in a safe place.

☐ When using your credit card at the credit gas pumps in use at several self-service stations, always take your receipt when you finish pumping your gas.

☐ Don't leave your card unattended in a place where it may be stolen, such as in your car, hotel room, office, or grocery cart.

☐ When you receive an updated card, immediately sign the new one and put it away. Cut up your old card before you throw it out.

NIGHTCLUBS AND BARS

Preventive Measures

☐ Pay your own way in bars.

☐ Don't carry a lot of cash.

☐ Don't get drunk.

☐ Don't give out personal information. If you want to see a person again, make a date to meet someplace, or give that person your work number.

☐ Keep your possessions in your hand or leave them with someone you trust, regardless of whether you're going to the bathroom, dancing, or getting cigarettes.

☐ Don't accept rides from strangers, and don't offer strangers rides.

☐ Don't leave the bar with anyone you don't feel completely safe with.

RECREATIONAL AREAS—PARKS AND BEACHES

Preventive Measures

☐ Avoid using public rest rooms alone.

☐ Leave at home expensive items and anything you don't really need.

☐ Know where the ranger or lifeguard station is.

☐ Avoid recreational areas at night. Too much criminal activity goes on there.

PUBLIC TRANSPORTATION

In metropolitan areas, using public transportation is often the easiest and quickest way to move from one part of the city to another. It's also environmentally "correct" because it helps decrease the number of cars on the road, but you need to make sure that it's a safe environment for you. While you cannot control who rides buses, subways, and trains, you can control what, when, and where you will ride and how you will react to any threatening situations aboard public transportation.

Juvenile delinquents and other criminals use public transportation, making it less safe, especially after dark. Records indicate that 1.3 percent of violent crimes take place on mass transit and that 1.6 percent of rapes occur on public transportation.

Preventive Measures

At the Bus Stop or Train Station

☐ When you use public transportation, arrange for a friend to meet you. Or get off first or walk with the crowd. Being a straggler makes you vulnerable to attack.

❑ Wait for your bus at a populated, well-lighted bus stop.

❑ Get a bus schedule and plan to arrive only a few minutes before the bus is due.

❑ When waiting for public transportation, don't stand too close to where the bus or subway train will be. Purse snatchers sometimes reach out the window and grab a purse as the bus or train is leaving.

❑ When waiting, turn around from time to time to see who is near you.

❑ At night don't stand inside a bus shelter; you want to be able to see and be seen by passersby.

❑ When waiting for a train or subway, stand near the ticket taker or ticket booth.

❑ In a subway station, take a look before you enter a corridor or tunnel to make sure no one is loitering there. If you are there at an off hour, wait until other people arrive before you enter.

❑ Have your change or token ready when you board.

❑ Avoid using the terminal's public bathrooms, where hoods congregate.

❑ Do not roam or leave the terminal while waiting for your transportation.

❑ Do not fall asleep in bus or train terminals.

❑ If you're bumped while waiting, check your belongings first, then look to see who might have bumped you.

❑ Carry loose change that you can drop if you are bumped or grabbed in a crowded area. People will look around to see whose money dropped, and the attention is likely to thwart your would-be assailant.

☐ Vary your routine so that it's less likely someone will confront you on your way to or from the bus or subway.

On the Bus, Subway, or Train: In the System

☐ Sit in front near the driver when you ride the bus. If that's not possible, choose an aisle seat next to the exit, so you can get off quickly if anyone bothers you—but take extra precautions with your purse.

☐ On a subway or train, sit in a car that has the driver, a conductor, or a security guard.

☐ Try not to be alone on public transportation with a man or a group of men.

☐ If someone touches you in a sexual way while you are traveling on public transportation, move to another part of the bus or train. If it's too crowded to do that, put your purse or packages between you and the molester. Trying to embarrass the person by making loud comments holds the potential of flipping out a mentally imbalanced offender. Play it safe.

☐ If anyone bothers you on a bus, ask the driver to drop you at a safe place.

☐ Keep your purse or briefcase on your lap with your hands on it when you ride public transportation.

☐ On the train, move forward if your car empties.

☐ On the train or subway, avoid the last car.

☐ If you are being verbally harassed, ignore it.

☐ Do not let yourself be surrounded by hoods on public transportation. Get up and move toward the exit.

☐ When the train approaches your station, walk to the car nearest the exit.

❏ If you are about to get off a train and a gang is about to get on, wait until the group is aboard and the doors are about to close before getting off so the people can't change their minds and follow you. Push your way off, if necessary, or run to another car.

❏ If you are being bothered on the car, avoid getting off at deserted stations, even if it means going out of your way. When you get off, go to the ticket booth, where the attendant can call security or the police for you.

❏ If you are attacked on the train, do not pull the emergency cord, which would stop the train and possibly prolong the attack.

Getting Off

❏ If you get off at a bus stop and find there are threatening people lurking nearby, stay at the bus stop. Look at your watch as if you are expecting someone to pick you up. Survey the scene. Is there someplace safer you can get to? If not, wait at the bus stop until you can take a taxi to your destination or until the danger passes.

❏ See who else is getting off when you do. It may be safer to go to the next stop.

❏ Familiarize yourself with the subway areas you use—where the phones are, which exits are locked at what times, and so forth.

Riding public transportation is usually an inexpensive, easy way to travel. Make sure it's safe as well.

If Anything Happens

❏ Report it to the police.

❏ If it happens in a store or mall, report it to the management and to mall security.

☐ If it takes place while you're riding a bus or subway, report it to public transportation authorities.

☐ If your purse or wallet is stolen, insist that store or mall personnel help you look for it. The purse or wallet, once emptied of cash, is often discarded right away.

☐ If your purse or briefcase is stolen with your ID and keys in it, change your locks. Also report the theft to your credit card issuers.

Not every plan will work, but if you have a plan, you increase your chances that you will arrive home safe and sound.

4

STREET CRIMES

ROBBERY

Jeff B., a college student in Philadelphia, liked to ride his bicycle aimlessly through the city as he relaxed. One day he realized that he had been riding longer than he had thought—it was dusk already—and he had ridden into a rough section of Philly. He decided to cut through a park to get back to campus. A moment later, however, he had to stop pedaling when he was surrounded by teenagers. "Hey," one of them said. "That's my bike."

"No, it's not," Jeff said, gripping the handlebars tighter.

"Yeah, it is," chimed in the others, and Jeff saw the flash of a knife. He kept his grip.

The only reason he has scars on his arm and back, he says now, instead of being dead, is that a police car rolled up unexpectedly and the gang scattered.

Robbery is *when a person takes money or property away from your care, custody, or control by force, threat, or intimidation.* Mugging is robbery.

Your first security rule is to avoid situations conducive to being robbed. You can pay dearly for not paying attention on the streets. For example, cutting through a city park at dark is asking for trouble, because hoods are known to hang out there.

Your second vital rule is if you are confronted by a robber, give him what he wants. As Jeff learned, if you don't follow a robber's orders, the crime is likely to escalate from robbery to assault or murder.

Robbery accounts for 5 percent of all the crimes in the FBI's *Crime Index,* and in 1991 it made up 36 percent of the violent crimes. Robberies took place most frequently in October and December and least often in April, at least in 1991. Statistics show that you are three times more likely to be confronted by a criminal at night—usually at 11 P.M.—than during the day.

Overall, in 1991, rural and suburban areas saw a greater increase in robberies than did cities. But cities with 1 million or more inhabitants had the highest rate of robbery—1,189 per 100,000 people.

Fifty-six percent of robberies took place on the street or highway, with the Northeast being a little riskier in this category than the rest of the nation (64.8 percent).

In 1991, 40 percent of the robbers employed firearms; 40 percent of the robbers depended on strong-arm tactics; 11 percent used knives.

Of those arrested in 1991 for robbery, 62 percent were younger than 25, and 91 percent were males. Sixty-one percent were African American, 38 percent were white; the rest were of other races.

"Larceny-theft" is how the FBI characterizes such crimes as shoplifting, pocket picking, purse snatching, thefts from motor vehicles, thefts of motor vehicles parts and accessories, and other crimes that don't involve force, violence, or fraud. The nation has seen a 9 percent rise in such incidents from 1987 to 1991—or a 5 percent increase in rate per 100,000 people.

The loss to victims nationwide was $3.9 billion for 1991. This is considered a low estimate, since many smaller stolen items are not reported to the police. Below are average losses of goods and property reported stolen as a result of

pocket picking	$366
purse snatching	$280
thefts from buildings	$788
thefts from motor vehicles	$544
thefts of motor vehicle accessories	$305
thefts of bicycles	$233

Thefts of motor vehicle parts, accessories, and contents made up the largest portion of reported larcenies at 37 percent.

(See VEHICLE THEFT.)

Street crime occurs most often in places where the attacker can isolate his target and cut down the chances of resistance and detection. Deserted side streets fall into this category. Studies indicate that in urban areas most robberies and purse snatchings take place downtown, a few blocks away from the commercial district. Nearly one-third of the robberies of the elderly are committed in the immediate vicinity of the victim's home and another third within the neighborhood.

Large parks and parking lots are also high-risk areas in a city. In public buildings, isolated areas—stairwells, corridors, elevators, and roofs—are high-risk crime locations. Think twice about venturing into alleys, paths, shortcuts, or around thick bushes and trees.

The way you dress, walk, and conduct yourself sends a message to others on the street. You want your message to be "I am not vulnerable." Here's how you transmit that message.

Dress in clothes that suit the area you're in. You don't wear obviously expensive clothes or jewelry in a rundown area. Doing so would send the signal that you have something worth stealing. You wear clothes and shoes that allow you to run if necessary. If you're a woman and you're going to be walking, don't wear seductive clothing. Unfortunate though it may be, some men take sexy clothes as a sign that you will welcome sexual attention.

Keep your head up when you are walking. Pay attention to where you are and what—and who—is in the vicinity. Do not be distracted by thinking about what you'll need to do when you get to your destination. Do not walk along reading a book. Do not just stare at the sidewalk a few feet ahead of you. You need to pay attention to what's going on around you and to potential hazards. For example, is an upcoming bush big enough to conceal an attacker? Is anyone approaching you from any direction?

Look at people around you. Don't be antagonistic; but depending on the situation, let them know that you have noted them. Brief eye contact with someone who is looking at you lets the other person know that you are paying attention. And criminals generally want to avoid attention. They don't want to be noticed, and they don't want to worry about being identified later on. Do the people look like they belong there? Is a man standing by a ladies' rest room waiting for his date, or is he waiting to follow someone inside and attack her? A little suspicion can help you be more prepared in case you are accosted.

Follow your instincts. If something in a scene doesn't feel right to you, move away from it or wait until the scene changes. If you're heading out to the parking lot, for example, and you're not comfortable with a crowd of young men you see in the lot, it is OK to wait until they've moved on, to wait till someone else is going to the parking lot, or to ask for an escort (if you're in a mall or business office).

If you can't find a way to prevent a confrontation with a robber, give him what he wants. Be especially compliant if he has a weapon. How you react often determines how you will fare in the confrontation. A Denver Anti-Crime Council study showed that people who resisted robbers were 3.7 times more likely to be hurt than victims who cooperated. The rationale is, by resisting you justify the mugger's meeting force with force; the robber believes you deserve the punishment you are getting. Any resistance gives him the provocation to vent his anger or to trigger irrational violence.

Decide how you will defend yourself if you are attacked. Carrying a weapon is dangerous: it can be wrestled away and used against you. If you're not willing to use a weapon, it's pointless to carry one. You also have to be aware that using deadly force is illegal if it is not clear that your attacker is going to kill you or assault you if you don't kill him first.

Other weapons also have their drawbacks. Carrying chemical sprays may be illegal in your area; they must be out and pointed in the right direction to be effective; they don't work if the wind is going in the wrong direction; and, as with other weapons, they can be taken from you and used against you.

Perhaps just as effective and safer to use are such homemade implements as a plastic lemon filled with lemon juice, vinegar, or hot sauce to squirt into an assailant's eyes. Or keep any sharp object—hat pin, screw, key, or pencil—ready to cut, scratch, and poke any assailant.

Preventive Measures

☐ Look like you know where you're going.

☐ Do not go out by yourself alone more than you have to.

☐ If you have to walk regularly at night, vary your course to decrease the odds of someone lying in wait for you, particularly on nights when you might be suspected of carrying more cash, such as payday.

☐ Vary your routine occasionally as well. The more predictable you are, the easier you make it for a robber to plan how to attack you.

☐ When you use public transportation, arrange for a friend to meet you when you leave the system. Or get off first or walk with the crowd. Being a straggler makes you vulnerable to attack.

☐ When waiting for public transportation, don't stand too close to where the bus or subway train will be. Purse snatchers sometimes reach out the window and grab a purse as the bus or train is leaving.

☐ Sit in front near the driver when you ride the bus.

☐ If possible plan your errands for the morning, rather than late afternoon or at night.

☐ Be extra cautious at night.

☐ Keep to well-lighted sidewalks and streets when you are walking or driving at night.

☐ Carry a small flashlight in your pocket or purse to help you find your keys or the lock as you reach your car or home.

☐ Be more cautious on the first and fifteenth of the month and on Thursdays or Fridays. Robbers know this is when people are often paid and more likely to be carrying large sums of money.

☐ Arrange to have your paycheck or social security checks deposited directly into your bank.

☐ If your employer won't do direct deposits, go with fellow employees to the bank; there's safety in numbers.

☐ Avoid letting strangers see how much money you have. Before you go shopping, try to determine how much money you'll need and put this amount in your pocket. Pay with this money instead of displaying the contents of your wallet or purse to any strangers.

☐ Note places along routes that you travel regularly where you can go in an emergency: police or fire stations, police call boxes and public telephones, stores that stay open late, and buildings with doormen.

☐ Avoid high-crime areas, if possible.

❏ Dress in a way that won't attract attention. Don't wear flashy clothing or jewelry in neighborhoods you don't know. Avoid clothing that can hinder your ability to run or defend yourself, such as high heels or tight skirts for women.

❏ Avoid wearing anything around your neck that could be used to grab or choke you, such as necklaces and scarves.

❏ Avoid eye and physical contact with gangs and other people loitering in public places. Particularly with gangs, it's better not to do anything that could be construed as provoking a confrontation.

❏ Don't be drunk in public.

❏ Avoid people who are drunk or high on drugs.

❏ Steer clear of liquor stores or bars where idle groups congregate.

❏ Have your keys out and ready when you get to your home or car. Once inside your home or car, immediately close and lock the door behind you.

❏ If you are being dropped off by a friend or taxi, ask the driver to wait until you are inside before he leaves. You can flash a light on and off to indicate you are inside and OK.

When Walking Alone

❏ Walk with a purpose and at a steady pace. Stand up straight and keep your head erect.

❏ Walk on the outside edge of the sidewalk, away from building entrances and alleys. Or walk in the middle of the sidewalk if parked cars on the street side offer robbers hiding places. If both sides of the sidewalk provide a criminal with cover, opt for the middle of the street.

☐ Walk against the flow of traffic so you won't be caught unaware by someone driving up from behind you.

☐ Carry a flashlight when walking after dark. Check the walkways around you; use the light to check the inside of your car. If you are confronted, you can shine the light into the assailant's eyes and jab him in the face with it.

☐ If you must walk past a group of people, cross the street to avoid the group or at least walk around it rather than through it.

☐ If you're coming up on a parked car that is occupied and has its motor running, cross the street to avoid passing close by it.

☐ Don't let strangers engage you in conversation as you're walking along. Answer any question they may have approached you with while you continue walking.

If You're Being Followed

☐ Look to see who is behind you. Cross the street, walk a few seconds, and look again. Your options are: Approach someone for help; go into a safe place; use a police call box or pay phone; walk in the middle of the street; or look for an unlocked parked car that you can climb into, lock the doors, and honk the horn.

☐ Drop your wallet into a mailbox. This is technically illegal—only mail is supposed to be deposited into mailboxes—but the postmaster usually cooperates and returns the wallet to you.

☐ If you are in a residential area, run to a house that looks occupied, and pound on the door. Even if the resident doesn't let you in, he can call the police. Ask him to leave the outside light on while he calls for help.

❑ If you think danger is imminent, try to attract attention. If you scream, yell "Fire!" Or use a good police whistle.

❑ If you use a police whistle, have it readily available in your jacket pocket, on a bracelet where it is handy, or on a necklace that breaks away so an assailant cannot use it to choke you.

❑ Consider using an air horn, a mechanical device that produces an earsplitting noise when activated. Carry it in your hand so you can activate it easily.

Wallets and Purses

❑ Pay by check or credit card to avoid carrying much cash on you. Buy traveler's checks if you can't stand to be without ready cash.

❑ Keep your cash separate from your credit cards.

❑ Men should carry their wallets or money clips in their front pants pocket or inside jacket pocket. A money belt offers the best security.

❑ Don't put your wallet in your rear pants pocket. A button is not a deterrent; the thief can easily slit open the bottom of the pocket to circumvent the button.

❑ If you insist on carrying your wallet in your rear pants pocket, buy a wallet that is longer than it is wide. Slip it into your pocket the long way, then turn it 90 degrees. This way no one can pull it out easily.

❑ When your wallet's in your front pants pocket, don't check it constantly to see if it's still there. Repeatedly patting your wallet (1) shows a pickpocket where it is and (2) sends a message that it contains something worth stealing. If you are jostled, however, press your hand against the wallet. This should protect you against pickpocketing.

☐ Don't be distracted by a chirping, hissing, or faint whistling—common devices of the pickpocket meant to draw your attention in one direction while his fingers work from the other side. Check your pockets immediately and look around accusingly, even if your wallet is still there.

☐ Be suspicious any time you are bumped or jostled in a public place, whether it's while someone is asking you to read a price tag for her in a store, while you're waiting for a bus, while someone is exiting an elevator, or some other situation. Pickpockets want your attention to be diverted—often by a cohort's actions—so they can steal your wallet.

☐ Report a pickpocketing to store security or police immediately. Often the thief will discard the wallet, minus cash and credit cards, in a rest room trash can soon after he has lifted your wallet. If so, it saves you the inconvenience of replacing all your other documents, such as your driver's license.

☐ Some people carry a "mugger's wallet"—one that contains a few dollar bills, an old ID that doesn't have a current address, and perhaps some expired credit cards. They keep this wallet where they normally carry a wallet. They then put their valuables in a separate place.

☐ Carry a few coins separate from your wallet or purse so you can make an emergency phone call if necessary.

☐ Women, avoid carrying a purse if possible.

☐ Examine the catch on your purse to see if it has weakened with age. You don't want your purse yawning open when you're not paying attention.

☐ Don't carry a wallet in a purse that opens at the top. Use a handbag that has a flap.

☐ Always keep your purse zipped or fastened.

☐ If you carry a purse, keep it close to your body, gripping it under your arm or with your hand. Put the strap across your body, with the purse's flap toward you.

☐ Don't wrap a purse strap around your wrist. Doing so is likely to leave you injured if a thief grabs your purse and gives you a shove.

☐ If you carry a purse with a coat or shawl, put the purse between the coat or shawl and your body.

☐ If you carry a purse and packages or books, place your purse between them and your body.

☐ A strapless purse, or one with a very short strap, should be carried like a football, tucked into your elbow close to your body, clasp side down. If a thief does try to grab it, release the clasp and let the contents spill out. A thief usually won't stop to sort through the mess.

☐ Always keep your purse in sight. Don't hang it on the back of your chair or put it on the floor or another chair.

☐ Keep your purse on your lap with your hands on top of it when you ride public transportation or go to the movies.

☐ When you go to the bathroom, keep your purse on your lap as much as possible.

☐ Carry your keys separate from your handbag.

☐ If your purse does get stolen, and both keys and ID cards are in the bag, have your locks at home changed immediately.

When Exercising

☐ Be alert.

☐ Exercise during daylight hours.

☐ Exercise with a companion. Don't let your companion straggle behind or get ahead of you.

☐ Avoid very loose clothing; it's easier for attackers to grab.

☐ If you wear glasses, wear them while you're exercising outside. You want to see potential trouble coming so you can avoid it.

☐ Stay away from high-crime areas or places where criminals are known to hang out, like public parks.

☐ Stay away from paths that take you through wooded areas or by isolated areas next to rivers. Such places offer attackers excellent concealment.

☐ Don't wear an expensive watch or jewelry likely to catch a mugger's eye.

☐ Carry an ID card but preferably one that doesn't have your home address. That way a mugger can't keep you detained while an associate goes to clean out your house.

☐ If someone looks like trouble, run away before the person can get close enough to confront you.

☐ If you're biking and someone tries to stop you, keep pedaling, even if you knock the person over. You're safer on your bike.

☐ Jog against traffic.

☐ Avoid headphones.

☐ Start your exercise routine in the spot that's least secure—the most deserted spot, the area with the worst visibility, or whatever. You're likely to be freshest and most able to outrun trouble at the beginning of your run or ride.

☐ Carry change to make emergency phone calls.

If Confronted by a Robber

☐ Don't resist.

☐ Remain as calm as you can. The time for screaming and running is before the confrontation. If you're face-to-face with a mugger, do not resist. Trying to run away during a robbery can increase your chances of being injured fivefold, according to a Denver Anti-Crime Council study.

☐ Do exactly what the robber tells you to do. You do not want to provoke the robber into attacking you, and you don't want to lose your life along with your property.

☐ Avoid sudden movements.

☐ Keep your hands out of your pockets or purse until the robber tells you otherwise.

☐ Respond promptly to instructions. Not responding or not responding fast enough counts as resistance.

☐ Don't scream unless help is near or unless the robber is obviously going to attack you. Screaming can anger your assailant and provoke him into injuring you.

☐ Don't try to run away unless the robber is next to you (close enough to incapacitate him in some way before you make a run for it), unless you are sure that safety is near, or unless you are being attacked. There's no point in running if the robber is going to catch up with you before you reach a safe haven. For most women, many men can run faster and longer so that safe haven needs to be within fifty feet.

☐ Don't say anything antagonistic, such as, "I'll never forget your face."

☐ Try a rational approach, such as suggesting that the robber keep your money but return your driver's license. The idea is that this indicates you understand how this scenario works and that you intend to go along.

❑ Try to register details about the robber that you can report to the police. Concentrate on physical details—eye color, height, weight, age, race, hair color, tattoos, birthmarks, or scars—instead of on his clothes, which are easily changed.

❑ If the mugger threatens you and you're alone, pretend to have some ailment. Say you have a heart condition, say you are pregnant, or act insane. If people are approaching, pretend to faint.

If Attacked

❑ Don't try to outfight the assailant. Remember that the goal of self-defense in this case is escape, not victory.

❑ Employ simple self-defense techniques, several of which are listed here:

- Concentrate on your attacker's most vulnerable areas: eyes, ears, nose, upper lip, groin, throat, kneecaps, and instep.
- Scratch, bite, and gouge.
- Kicking is better than hitting because you can deliver a harder blow with your foot than with your fist. You should not stand back, however, to try to kick him. The person will move away, turn your blows away, or grab your foot. The most damage can be done close-up.
- Use anything handy as a defensive weapon. The possibilities include books, a rolled-up newspaper, an umbrella, your purse, keys, a lit cigarette, a comb, sharp pencil, pen, fingernail file, kitchen utensils (for example, a fork, bottle opener, corkscrew), or aerosol containers (the last are awk-

ward to manage and have the same drawbacks as chemical sprays).

- If you use keys, put a key between your thumb and index finger or put two or three keys between your fingers and wrap your fingers around the remaining keys on your key ring. Hold your fist sideways and jab the keys into the eyes or face of your attacker. Rake the keys down sideways; otherwise the keys may slip backward into your fingers.

- Use your head to butt your attacker on the forehead, nose, mouth, or chin. Use either the front of the forehead or the back of your head. Be sure your teeth are clenched together and that your mouth is firmly shut.

  If you are attacked from the front and your assailant grabs your wrists, move your arms up and out, putting pressure against his thumbs to break his grip.

- If a person tries to hit you, use your arms to block the blows. If your attacker has a knife, you can use a purse or coat rolled around your arm to protect yourself.

- If you are being choked from the front, try to break the hold by lifting your arms up and around the outside of the attacker's arms, then thrust your hands as hard as possible in the assailant's elbows as you pull away. To try to disable the assailant, take a step forward and slam your knee into his crotch, aiming for his testicles.

- If an attacker puts his arms around your neck from behind, maneuver for air first. Do this by turning your head toward his elbow. Grab one of his fingers and bend it back as hard as you can. If you cannot get away, stomp on the top of his foot with your heel. Fourteen pounds of pressure breaks the bones in the foot, so even if you are small, this should cause your assailant considerable pain. As a last resort, reach down with your hand and grab the person's testicles. A hard squeeze or pull should put your assailant into shock.

- Bite any flesh within reach.
- Try to kick him in the spine.
- Canes and umbrellas can be used to defend yourself. Aim for the nose with a cane. Try to thrust an umbrella into the assailant's eyes or throat.

☐ Scream as you try to run away.

☐ If you can't run away, do whatever you can to defend yourself, screaming the entire time.

☐ Tell the assailant when he has hurt you, in an attempt to keep him from dehumanizing you and hurting you worse.

☐ If you can't escape the beating, curl into a ball on the ground with your arms protecting your head and your knees tucked up to your stomach to protect your vital organs.

☐ Consider carrying Mace or other chemicals. A green-dye spray called DYEWitness temporarily blinds the assailant and leaves his skin and clothing green for a week. It also leaves a trail of green droplets that police can trace. It can be used up to seven feet away and does not require a permit.

If Mugged

☐ When the mugger leaves, see which way the thief goes and if he enters a building or vehicle. If he uses a car, try to see the car's make, model, and license plate.

☐ Write down what you remember of the incident so you can give an accurate account to the police.

☐ Call the police right away. If a crime is reported within two minutes, it greatly improves the odds that the police can apprehend the thief. After that, odds decline unless you can supply a detailed description of the offender.

❏ Report the theft to your insurance company.

❏ If you were assaulted as well as robbed, check into victim's compensation. Contact your police office or district attorney's office to find out if your state has a victim compensation program that would cover medical costs and loss of earnings if you are eligible. Generally:

- The crime must be reported within seventy-two hours.
- The victim can't be breaking the law himself.
- The victim must not have provoked the crime that injures him (for example, being drunk in public or hitchhiking).
- The victim must cooperate with authorities by giving statements, prosecuting, and so forth.
- The victim must have genuine financial need. He is not eligible if he can afford to pay his medical bills.

❏ Change your locks if the robber got your keys and ID card with your address. Tell the police if the thief got both.

❏ Notify your credit card companies by phone and in writing.

❏ If you have had your purse or wallet stolen, check nearby trash cans, bushes, alleys, and rest rooms to see if the thief has discarded what he doesn't want of your possessions. Also contact your local postmaster to see if your purse or wallet has turned up in a mailbox. Occasionally thieves send them back, courtesy of the postal service.

If You Witness an Attack

❏ Call—or send someone else to call—for the police. Sometimes a team of assailants acts out an attack to sucker in a good Samaritan. Call for help, then intervene only if you're sure you're not endangering yourself.

❏ If you need to summon the police, dial 0 and say, "Emergency—police." Find out if your community uses 911.

RAPE

Being raped ranks as one of the leading fears women have. In a 1992 survey of readers, *McCall's* magazine found that fear of rape was second after the fear of being hit by a drunk driver.

What are a woman's chances of being raped during her lifetime? It depends on how you define rape, if you base the statistic on reported rapes only, and what sample population you use. Estimates for rape and attempted rape have ranged from 24 to 63 percent of all women. But in 1992, the National Women's Study—a government-financed, independently conducted study of more than four thousand American women that covered three years—was released. It calculated the incidence of more than just reported rapes or vaginal or penile rapes. The picture it draws of rape in America looks like this:

It defines rape as *"an event that occurred without the woman's consent, involved the use of force or the threat of force, and involved sexual penetration of the victim's vagina, mouth or rectum."* The study indicated that 13 percent of women surveyed were the victim of at least one completed rape. Attempted rapes were not covered by the study.

Many women worry most about being raped by a stranger. But almost half of the rapes reported for all age groups were committed by someone the victim knew.

The study revealed that 75 percent of the victims were raped by people they knew well: 45 percent were assaulted by friends, relatives, or neighbors; 11 percent by fathers or stepfathers; 10 percent by boyfriends or ex-boyfriends; and 9 percent by husbands or ex-husbands. Three percent did not categorize the identity of the rapist.

Unfortunately, women who are raped by an acquaintance are often raped more than once by the same person. Victims of a stranger usually suffer the crime once.

The FBI defines rape simply as *"the carnal knowledge of a female forcibly and against her will."* Keeping count by this definition, reported rapes rose by 3 percent from 1990, and 13 percent since 1987. But many organizations believe that the FBI's definition is too simplistic and that rape is one of the most unreported crime in the nation.

Geographically, the highest rate of reported rape, for 1991 occurred in the West, with 91 victims per 100,000 females. The Midwest had a rate of 89 per 100,000; the South, 88; and the Northeastern states, 57. The Midwest had the greatest increase i rate. In terms of metropolitan areas versus rural ones, an averag of 91 women out of 100,000 were assaulted in metropolitan area 67 per 100,000 in cities outside metropolitan areas, and 46 pe 100,00 in rural counties. The greatest rate increase—71 percent— took place in cities outside metropolitan areas.

Women who are single or poor are at the highest risk. Rape vic tims are most often between twelve and thirty-four, with wome sixteen to nineteen being the most vulnerable. But girls as youn as four and women in their eighties and nineties have been rape Ten percent of all reported rapes involve women who hitchhike Incidentally, two tenths of 1 percent of rape victims are male.

Statistics indicate that a rapist is almost always the same race a his victim, but interracial rape may be as underreported as rap itself.

More rapes occur at home than anywhere else, because this sta tistic includes marital, acquaintance, or stranger rapes occurring i the home and in college dormitories. Reported rapes take place a home (35 percent); on the street (19.9 percent); at or near a friend home (10.5 percent); near home (10.3 percent); in a commercia building (7.9 percent); in a parking lot or garage (3.4 percent); o public transportation (1.6 percent); in a bar or nightclub (1.5 per cent); and such places as apartment-building yards, librarie churches, playgrounds, hospitals, and parks (9.9 percent), accorc ing to the Bureau of Justice Statistics.

Reported attacks happen most frequently in the evening, a night, and during the weekend. More rapes are reported durin the summer than any other season.

Resisting rape can help, according to statistics compiled by th Bureau of Justice Statistics. By resisting in some way, 38.8 avoide injury or greater injury, 37.4 percent enabled themselves to escape, and 21.5 percent scared off the offender. But 18.9 percent who resisted found that it made the situation worse.

According to the statistics, women resisted physically (20.8 percent), by screaming or getting help (19.6 percent), by appeasing the offender or persuading him not to attack (18.7 percent), or by running away or hiding (13 percent). Others scared off their offender (for example, by threatening to call the police); attacked or threatened the offender without a weapon (7.9 percent); attacked the offender with a weapon (0.8 percent), or used some other method (6.2 percent).

The largest percentage of single-offender rapes are committed by white men in their twenties. Another study found that just under 50 percent of convicted rapists had been previously arrested and booked for a crime. Seventy-one percent of the rapes were planned, and another 11 percent were partially planned. That is, the rapist decided to rape a woman but wasn't specific about whom he thought he would rape.

Different studies have found varying rates of rape being committed by two or more assailants. A Toronto study found 50 percent of rapes were committed by groups; another found 43 percent were; and a Washington, D.C., study put the rate of occurrence at 18.5 percent.

Alcohol is often involved in the crime. Rapists who had been drinking right before an attack completed the crime 80 percent of the time, compared with 58 percent by nondrinkers. One study (Queen's Bench, an organization of women lawyers in San Francisco) found that 61.6 percent of rapists had been drinking immediately before the assault.

Knowing these facts about when, where, and by whom rape is committed can help you cut your chances of being sexually assaulted. It gives you notice about what to avoid and when to be particularly careful. Below are suggestions on avoiding a confrontation with a rapist, what to do if threatened with rape, possible self-defense moves, and what to do if you were raped.

Preventive Measures

☐ Make your home as secure as possible against intruders (*See* *AT HOME*). According to the Rape Crisis Center of Washington, D.C., about half of all rapes take place in the home; half of all rapes are committed by someone the victim knows; 60 percent of all rapes are planned, and two thirds of all convicted rapists are married men who have been having regular intercourse with a willing partner.

☐ Lock the doors and windows of your home and car.

☐ Pay attention to your surroundings and anyone in it constantly.

☐ Be sure no strangers are near your car—and that includes under it—when you approach it.

☐ Carry your keys in your hand, ready to get into your car or into your home.

☐ Look inside your car before getting in.

☐ Be suspicious of any action that is out of the ordinary. For example, people usually sit in seats surrounded by empty seats on a bus. If someone passes by an empty row to sit down next to you, it's cause for suspicion.

☐ Do not feel you can trust someone you don't really know simply because you work together or attend the same school.

☐ Do not walk home alone if you are not going to be paying attention. If you are lost in melancholy, angry, or have been drinking or taking drugs, find a friend to accompany you. You should not be distracted and self-absorbed.

☐ When you are waiting on the street for transportation, stand so you are balanced and ready to move if necessary.

❏ Dress modestly if you're going to be walking on the street alone. It is the painful truth that some men see provocative dress as an invitation to sex. Wear clothes and shoes that allow you to run and defend yourself if necessary.

❏ Don't flirt or tease with strangers.

❏ Put only your last name on your mailbox.

❏ Consider getting a dog.

❏ If you are home alone and a stranger comes to your door, engage in a pretend conversation with a male before you open the door even a crack.

❏ Don't let moving men or repair men know you are alone.

❏ Avoid dangerous areas, such as an isolated laundry room, especially at night.

❏ Stay off the roof of your apartment building and out of back stairwells.

❏ If a man calls with a wrong number, never give him your name and phone number. Instead, ask what number he is trying to reach.

❏ Avoid giving out any personal information over the phone. If a man calls and offers to give you a credit card from a store after you answer some personal questions, refuse. If you want the card, go apply in person.

❏ Use only an initial and your last name in the telephone book.

❏ Use your daytime office number to give to businesses that are unfamiliar to you. Make it clear to your fellow employees that they are not to divulge any personal information about you.

☐ If biking, use your detachable metal tire pump as a weapon by jabbing it into the attacker's stomach or swinging it like a club.

☐ If you've been out hiking with your boyfriend, still check the car before you get into it. There have been cases where the woman got into the car first and the rapist suddenly drove off, leaving the man by the side of the road. Then the offender drove to a secluded spot and raped the woman.

☐ If you're being followed and are in a neighborhood where houses have lights on, pretend to have arrived at your house. Look at an upstairs window and yell, "I'm home, George. Can you come open the door for me?"

Elevators

☐ Be wary of getting into an elevator with one or more men if you are the only woman.

☐ If you are in an elevator and someone suspicious gets on, get out and wait for the next elevator.

☐ In an elevator, stand next to the control panel and be ready to hit the alarm button and the buttons to all the floors. You want to make noise and be able to get off the elevator as soon as possible if something happens. Do not hit the stop button. You do not want to be trapped.

☐ Do not ride in an elevator if the roof escape hatch is ajar.

☐ Stand back from the door while you wait for the elevator's arrival so that you can't be easily pulled or shoved in.

☐ When getting off, look all the way around so that no one can come from behind and surprise you as you walk away.

Public Transportation

☐ If you are a woman and a man touches you while you are traveling on public transportation, move to another part of the bus or train. Trying to embarrass the man with loud comments holds the potential of flipping out a mentally imbalanced offender. Play it safe.

☐ Wait for your bus at a populated, well-lighted bus stop.

☐ On a bus, sit near the driver.

☐ If anyone bothers you on a bus, ask the driver to drop you at a safe place.

☐ When waiting for a train or subway, stand near the ticket taker or ticket booth.

☐ On a subway or train, sit in the car that has the driver, a conductor, or a security guard.

☐ Try not to be alone on public transportation with a man or a group of men.

☐ When the train approaches your station, walk to the car nearest the exit.

☐ If you are about to get off a train and a gang is about to get on, wait until the people are aboard and the doors are about to close before getting off so they can't change their minds and follow you. Push your way off or run to another car if necessary.

☐ If you are being bothered on the car, avoid getting off at deserted stations, even if it means going out of your way. When you get off, go to the ticket booth, where the attendant can call security or the police for you.

☐ If you are attacked on the train, do not pull the emergency cord, which would stop the train and possibly prolong the attack.

Your Car

☐ Always lock your car, when you are in it as well as when you leave it.

☐ Keep your car well maintained. Read and follow the recommended maintenance listed in the owner's manual. Have the oil and water checked every three or four weeks or more often if you drive a great deal.

☐ Keep the gas tank at least one-quarter full. Running out of gas is asking for trouble.

☐ Choose steel-belted radial tires (they're least likely to have flats or blowouts), and check them weekly for nails, glass, and cuts. Check the air in the tires frequently. Learn how to change a tire rapidly so you can get on your way again as quickly as possible after a flat.

☐ When you go out at night, tell a friend or relative where you're going and when you expect to return. If you are late coming back, someone can go looking for you.

☐ Park in a well-lighted, busy place as close to your destination as possible.

☐ If you think you are being followed in a car, try to elude the other car by changing directions, speeding up, or making a U-turn.

☐ If you are definitely being followed, honk your horn, drive to a police station or a gas station, and ask the attendant for help. Do not drive home. If you are in the country, keep honking as you drive to the nearest home. If possible, get the license plate number of the car following you and report it to the police.

☐ If a car following you flashes its lights, do not pull over. If it is a police officer who wants to pull you over, he will use a red or blue flashing light and his siren.

☐ Do not stop to help if you see a car that needs assistance along the side of the road. Instead, go to the nearest phone and call the police or highway patrol.

☐ If a man tries to enter your car while you are stopped at a light, honk your horn and, if possible, drive through the light.

☐ If someone does get into your car, do everything to avoid going to a secluded spot. Also, try to avoid letting him tie you up unless he has a weapon and threatens your life. Attract attention by driving through a red light, running into a parked car, or driving up on the curb.

Hitchhiking

☐ Do not hitchhike. Ten percent of rapes involved women who were hitchhiking.

☐ If you insist on hitchhiking, try to lower your chances of being raped by following this advice:

- Don't hitchhike alone. Hitchhiking with a man is safer than hitchhiking with a girlfriend.
- Don't accept a ride from a man, especially if he stops when you don't have your thumb out or if he changed directions in order to pick you up.
- Don't accept a ride from a car full of men. Never get into the backseat with a group of men.
- If you do accept a ride from a man, before you get in the car you should do the following: Look in the backseat to see if anyone is hiding there. Check to see if your door has a handle and that it works in case you need a quick exit. Check to see if the driver is exposing himself and where both his hands are. Turn down the ride if there is any evidence that he has been drinking.

- Always ask the driver where he is going. If he says "Wherever you want to go," it's the wrong answer. Turn him down.
- Know where you're going and about how long it should take to get there. If the driver starts heading the wrong way, insist on getting out immediately.
- Before the car picks up speed, open and close the door to make sure the driver can't control it.
- Weather permitting, ride with the window rolled down, in case you need to yell out of it.
- Ask to be dropped off a little way from your destination, especially if you are going home. Avoid letting strange men know where you live.
- Carry something that can be used as a defensive weapon, such as a purse with hard corners, a hardcover book, or a bottle.

If Confronted with a Rapist

The best thing to do is to avoid an actual confrontation with an attacker. If you have some sort of escape route—getting into your car, running back into a store, getting off the elevator—take it immediately. Don't quash your instinct to run away because you're afraid you're being paranoid.

If you can't avoid a confrontation, however, you should consider passive self-defense first. Size up each situation first to determine what tactic is likely to be successful. Fainting on a deserted jogging path where an assailant can drag you to a secluded spot isn't likely to be as effective as fainting in a crowded parking lot, where the attacker would have to actually pick you up and carry you someplace to avoid being detected.

The suggestions that follow include passive and aggressive resistance. Plan how you might react when face to face with an attacker. Try to be realistic, and take into account your personality and physical capabilities. Try to be flexible. You may have always thought you'd scream if someone jumped you, only to find that you can't make a sound when it happens. And if you can't get away, or if the assailant has a weapon, remember that your life is more important than anything else.

Passive Resistance

- [ ] Statistically, half the rapists run away when their intended victim screams; unfortunately, the other half becomes violent. If your attacker's first response is violent, that may cut off all your other options.

- [ ] Pretend to faint. Go totally limp and let your belongings fall where they may. If your attacker chooses your purse over you, fine. While he's distracted with that, you can consider getting up and running away. If you stay down, you do run the risk of being kicked before the assailant flees.

- [ ] Break open a vial of D-ter, a chemical that is supposed to smell so awful that anyone smelling it—you included—is likely to throw up. The notion is that the smell of D-ter and the sight of you vomiting will keep an attacker away from you.

- [ ] Urinate, defecate, or gag yourself to vomit.

- [ ] Talk. A rapist wants to see himself as the victor over you, his prey. What you want to do is to change his perception of himself and you. Some women have been able to talk potential rapists out of the attack. Others have played along with their attacker's demands until his guard was down and they could escape.

  One co-ed walking home late from the library was startled when a man stepped out from the bushes as she passed by on her way back to the dorm. "Oh," she said quickly, "I'm so glad to see you. I've been worried about having to walk home alone at night, and now I have some company to see me safely to my door. It's really great . . . ." On and on she rattled as she kept walking. The befuddled would-be attacker actually walked her as far as her dorm, where she started screaming and ran in to call campus security.

❑ Try to stay calm. Try to get him to see that you are both human beings.

❑ Promise to cooperate. He may let his guard down long enough for you to escape. But it may mean submitting to the rape if it is your only chance of survival. You must assess the situation and decide for yourself.

❑ Stall for time, in the hope that a means of escape will present itself. Plan how you might approach such a situation. You could tell the attacker that you have a sexually transmitted disease, such as AIDS.

❑ Feign madness by babbling in gibberish, making strange gestures with your hands, and so forth.

❑ Force yourself to say, "No, not here. Let's go over there and I'll give you the most incredible sex." The idea is that the attacker will be so astonished by this response that he'll drop his guard when he removes his pants, giving you the opportunity to run and scream for help.

❑ Don't struggle in situations where resistance is going to result in a severe beating or in your death.

❑ Assume he is stronger and faster than you are. Act accordingly. Don't try to outfight or outrun him; this will likely result in a beating.

❑ When possible, try to control your breathing by inhaling through your nose and exhaling slowly through your mouth. This will help you feel more in control and can give you the edge you need to escape.

Aggressive Resistance

☐ Practice self-defense techniques.

☐ Fight dirty. Bite ends of fingers, toes, nose, ears, cheeks, and other sensitive spots; use your elbow on his ribs or jaw; scratch; jam thumbs into his neck; twist his ears, clap cupped hands over his ears to create a dizzying thunder.

☐ If you clap cupped hands over your attacker's ears, this can stun him, but this will not stop someone who is high (and incapable of feeling pain) or someone who has a high tolerance for pain. It is often better to kick his knee or groin, so that even if he doesn't feel pain, he is immobilized.

☐ If attacked in a business area and you're near a window with metal sensing tape indicating it is attached to an alarm, throw anything you can—a briefcase, a rock, a purse, or a shoe—through the glass.

☐ To try to escape a gang rape, try to separate the attackers. Say you want to enjoy each of them one at a time so you can get to know them. Then go with one person to a secluded spot and try to act against him. Try to determine the leader; if he is hurt or his plan is foiled, the others may be too confused to decide what to do. Try to convince the leader to be the first to "have you," go as far from the others as possible, and then try to escape.

☐ If gang rape is unavoidable, try to relax your body as much as possible to mitigate internal damage. Focus on the fact that you will live through it, you will get medical attention, and you will be all right. Concentrate on remembering as many details as you can—but don't mention that to your attackers, who may choose to kill you.

☐ While the attacker uses one hand to hold you and the other to undo his clothes and yours, you should concentrate all your attention on attacking his genitals with your hands, knees, or teeth by scratching, pulling, and hitting. Pulling hard on a man's testicles, for one, puts him into shock, giving the victim an opportunity to run away screaming.

❏ If an attacker brings up his knee to protect his genitals, kick his knee to immobilize him.

❏ Never carry a lethal weapon you're not prepared to use to the fullest extent. Nonlethal weapons are meant to cause enough injury to allow you to escape.

❏ If someone tries to force his way in your door, try poking his eyes and then shove his chin with the heel of your hand. Push his chin up and back, which should give you enough space and time to slam the door shut.

❏ If you wake up and someone is throttling you, smash down with your forearms on his elbow. Hit the tip of his nose if possible and keep hitting his face—and groin, if he covers his face—while you try to get up and escape.

❏ If he grabs your hair, clamp your hand on top of the attacker's. Press it firmly to your head, then rotate your head and body in the direction of the attacker's little finger to break his hold.

❏ If you're grabbed by the wrist, kick at the attacker's knee.

❏ Use your arms to defend against blows with a club or board.

❏ If you're knocked to the ground, turn on your side and start kicking the assailant's shins, pivoting if the attacker moves around.

❏ Never fight an armed man unless it's clear that he's going to kill you afterward.

❏ Kick or hit the opponent's throat with an object or stiffened hand. A blow to the side of the neck can rupture a main artery; a sharp blow to the front can cause the larynx to swell, causing suffocation.

- [ ] Push your thumbs into his eyes. Moderate pressure will make him pass out; stronger pressure will kill him. Even a man wearing glasses will jerk back if you try to jab him in the eyes.

- [ ] Press your index fingers into his neck below the earlobes, just above the jawbone. Two seconds of firm pressing will put him into shock; six seconds into the morgue.

- [ ] Use an umbrella like a spear or sword, rather than like a club.

If your life is threatened, submit to the rape. If your attacker threatens you after the rape, however, fight with everything you've got.

If You Are Raped

- [ ] Get away from the attacker as quickly as you can.

- [ ] Don't clean yourself (don't shower, bathe, douche, or change clothes).

- [ ] Don't touch any smooth surfaces, such as telephones, at the scene of the attack that the rapist may have touched so that the police can dust for prints.

- [ ] Call the police.

- [ ] Call a rape crisis center and have someone go with you to the hospital. A rape crisis center can also advise you on how to keep the hospital examination and dealing with the police from being as traumatic as the rape itself.

- [ ] Call a friend or family member who can come and be with you.

☐ Try to recall all the details right away and record them so they can be used by the police.

☐ Go to the emergency room and make it clear that you are a rape victim so that you'll be attended to promptly. Take a change of clothes with you because the ones you're wearing will need to be kept as evidence.

☐ Have your own doctor present during the examination if you want.

☐ Get preventive treatment for sexually transmitted diseases and pregnancy.

☐ Even if you feel in control, don't be afraid to show your emotions or to act hysterical at first when you are questioned about the event. Doctors and police officers who are likely to testify if your rapist is brought to trial may be more convinced about the veracity of your account if you act like they think someone should act after such a traumatic event.

☐ Carefully consider prosecuting if the rapist is arrested. Going to trial means reliving the experience as you are asked to relate the details throughout the trial. But the hope is that you will punish a criminal *and* get him off the streets to keep yourself and others safe.

☐ Get counseling.

☐ If you are raped near or at home and the rapist is not caught right away, find a way to notify your neighbors so that they can be especially alert.

☐ Put an answering machine on your phone, and let it screen your calls. If the rapist calls, save the tape.

☐ Do not confront the rapist on your own. Tell the police if you think you may encounter your assailant again.

(See also AT HOME, OUT AND ABOUT, STREET CRIME: ROBBERY.)

STALKING

Stalking typically involves a woman who was once in an intimate relationship that has since turned sour. An estimated 75 to 80 percent of all stalking cases are rooted in a domestic context—relationships that have ended and one party won't accept the breakup. Only about 20 percent of stalking cases involve strangers, and those are usually people with severe mental illness.

Occasionally a jilted woman will stalk a man or his new girlfriend. But the majority of cases involve men stalking women.

Stalking is usually a process that escalates. The stalker may start out abusing his victim with harassing telephone calls that later become threatening. Then eventually the stalker—a boyfriend, a coworker, or even a stranger—shows up at his victim's house with a gun.

Stalking is such a problem that thirty-one states have passed anti-stalking laws.

Preventive Measures

☐ If the stalker calls you, do not talk to him. Hang up.

☐ If the calls continue, keep a log of the time, the date, and what the caller says. Then hang up or let an answering machine take the call. Save all tapes of the calls.

☐ If the calls continue for an extended period, get an unlisted number.

☐ If the calls are threatening, notify the police. If you know the individual that is harassing you, request a restraining order.

☐ Have the police conduct a home security check.

☐ If you have children, alert them to avoid the individual harassing you (assuming you know the individual).

☐ Alert your neighbors. Ask them to let you know if they see the individual in your neighborhood.

☐ Consider self-defense equipment and training.

(See AT HOME, OUT AND ABOUT.)

AGGRAVATED ASSAULT AND MURDER

More than half of the violent crimes reported to the FBI were **aggravated assaults,** which involves *one person attacking another with the intent of inflicting severe injury.* This sort of attack often employs a weapon or other means likely to kill or greatly harm the victim. The FBI counts attempts as well as completed assaults.

The South, which is the most populous region in the United States, accounted for 39 percent of the aggravated assault volume in 1991 (but the West has a higher per capita rate of 355 per 100,000), followed by 25 percent in the West, 20 percent in the Midwest, and 17 percent in the Northeast. Only the Northeast showed a decline from the previous year. Overall, however, such assaults were up 4 percent compared with 1990, with cities of populations from 250,000 to 499,999 registering the greatest increase, 8 percent.

Sixty percent of those arrested for committing aggravated assaults were white; 38 percent were African American; and other races made up the remainder. Eighty-six percent of these arrests were men.

According to the FBI, while total violent crime remained steady and assaults and rapes increased, murders declined by 6 percent during 1991. Estimated at 24,703 murders nationwide, more people were killed in August than any other month, and February had the least number of murders. In the nation's cities, the murder rate was up 6 percent, with the greatest increase registered in cities with populations of 50,000 to 99,999. Suburban counties saw a 2 percent rise in their murder volumes. Since 1982, their murder rate has risen 18 percent.

The South as a region had the highest rate of murders—12 per 100,000 people—followed by metropolitan areas, with 11 murders per 100,000 people. Rural counties registered a rate of 6 per 100,000, and cities outside metropolitan areas had the lowest per capita rate—5 for every 100,000.

According to the FBI's information, 78 percent of the murder victims were male, and 89 percent were aged eighteen or older. Half of these victims (48 percent) were twenty to thirty-four years old. Of those for whom race was known, an average of 50 percent of the victims were black; 47 percent were white. To a great degree, victims were killed by someone of the same race as themselves, and offenders were almost always men, regardless of the sex of the victim. Murderers used firearms—handguns, rifles, and shotguns—for seven out of ten murders committed.

Almost half of the murders in this country are committed by people who are related to or acquainted with the victim. Among female victims in 1991, 28 percent were slain by husbands or boyfriends, while only 4 percent of the men killed were done in by wives or girlfriends. Of the murders reported, most occurred as a result of arguments (32 percent); in connection with another crime, such as robbery or arson (21 percent), or during brawls while offenders were drunk or high (3 percent).

The chances that you might be murdered are slim, and they depend to a great degree upon your family, acquaintances, and lifestyle. Some people are raised in families that are violent; others live in neighborhoods that are more violent than others. Here are some ways, however, to decrease your chances of being murdered.

Preventive Measures

☐ Stay alert to any situations that might get out of hand, whether you're in a bar, on the street, or at home.

☐ Do not allow any firearms in your home.

☐ If firearms are in your home, store the ammunition separately from the weapon, and keep each locked up.

☐ Get family or marital counseling if you have a violent spouse, and consider moving out.

☐ Report it to the police if your former lover or spouse is stalking you.

☐ If someone with a weapon attempts to rob you, let him. Don't resist unless it is clear that he intends to kill you afterward.

☐ If someone with a weapon attempts to rape you, don't resist physically unless you can get him to put his weapon away. The only exception to that is if he clearly intends to kill you. Then you should fight with everything in you for a chance to escape.

☐ If you encounter a burglar in your home, get out of the way. Don't get between him and an exit. A panicked burglar can become a murderer.

☐ If you see someone being attacked, call the police. Lend assistance only if you will not put yourself in danger.

☐ Avoid confrontations with strangers. You don't know what you might be dealing with.

☐ Don't be confrontational with fellow employees. Let third parties handle any disputes so that the other employee can't hold you responsible for any disciplinary action that may be taken against him.

If Assaulted

☐ Call the police.

☐ See if you qualify for victim's compensation. Most victim compensation laws provide funds to victims of violent crimes or their survivors. The amount usually covers medical costs and loss of earnings. Only innocent victims are eligible; that is, if your negligence incited the crime, it may disqualify you. Unless property was lost during a physical attack, it is not reimbursed. Your police department or district attorney's office can tell you if you are eligible for your state victim compensation program. Generally,

- The crime must be reported within seventy-two hours.
- The victim can't be breaking the law himself.
- The victim must not have provoked the crime that injures him (for example, being drunk in public or hitchhiking).
- The victim must cooperate with authorities by giving statements, prosecuting, and so forth.
- The victim must have genuine financial need. He is not eligible if he can afford to pay his medical bills.

5

THE ELDERLY

Elderly people are the victims of more burglaries and swindles than violent crimes. Of the crimes committed against them, the elderly appear to be particularly susceptible to crimes motivated by economic gain such as robbery, personal and household larceny, and burglary. For example, those under age sixty-five are almost four times more likely to be assaulted than robbed, but for those sixty-five and older, the likelihood of assault is only 1.5 times that of robbery.

Most of the homicide victims over sixty-five were killed during a robbery. And robbery victims in that age group (83 percent) were more likely than any other group to be mugged by a stranger.

Elderly men are more likely to be subjected to violent crime and household crimes, but older women are more often victims of personal larceny with contact, that is, purse snatching. Elderly blacks are generally more likely than whites to suffer from a criminal act. Not surprisingly, those living in cities are the most vulnerable, but suburb dwellers experience higher rates of personal theft. Elderly folks in rural areas are more likely to experience household crimes in general, and burglary in particular, compared with their suburban counterparts. Securing their homes is especially important for older people, because the elderly are almost twice as likely to be robbed or assaulted at or near their homes.

Unfortunately, crimes against property—robberies, burglaries, and con games—can also be more troublesome for an older person living on a fixed income than for a younger person. And the psychological impact can be most devastating. Indeed, just worrying about crime is a major concern for the elderly, according to studies done by the American Association of Retired Persons (AARP). An AARP study conducted in Pennsylvania showed that one quarter of older citizens were afraid to go out once the schools in their area had dismissed. Half of those polled dared not go outside at night, and two thirds would not open their door to a stranger.

If an older person is injured during a crime, its impact is likely to be greater than it would be on a younger victim. Fourteen percent of elderly victims who are injured need hospital care, compared with 8 percent of younger victims.

Older women can take a small measure of comfort in the fact that fewer than 1 percent per thousand women aged sixty-five or older get raped. This statistic is meaningless, however, to the woman who is sexually assaulted.

Sadly, sometimes a relative or acquaintance victimizes an old person. This mistreatment can range from unintentional neglect, such as when a well-meaning caregiver simply cannot meet the older person's needs, to physical abuse. Intentional mistreatment results from greed, dysfunctional family stress, or other factors; the causes vary from individual to individual and case to case. We must recognize, however, that any mistreatment—not just physical abuse—of a frail elderly person can be very harmful. Certain states classify some forms of mistreatment as felonies. So just as an elderly person can take steps to protect himself from crime, he can and should work to protect himself from mistreatment.

Ways the elderly can prevent crime and mistreatment, both from strangers and acquaintances, include:

Preventive Measures

☐ Lock the doors and windows to your home.

☐ Lock your car.

☐ Be alert when approaching your car, since many robberies and assaults take place in or near cars.

☐ Have your social security checks deposited directly into your bank.

☐ Do not go out by yourself alone more than you have to. Find a group of friends to go out with you.

☐ Vary your routine occasionally. The more predictable you are, the easier you make it for a robber to plan how to attack you.

☐ Don't wear valuable jewelry every day. Keep it in a safety-deposit box and save it for special occasions.

☐ Pay by check or credit card to avoid having too much cash on you.

☐ Carry a small amount of cash to appease a robber if you do get confronted.

☐ Carry only the credit cards you plan to use.

☐ Carry your checkbook only when you plan to use it.

☐ Carry your cash in different places, for example, in your shirt and pants pockets. Make sure you have change for a phone call or bus fare tucked into a safe place.

☐ Carry only a one- or two-day supply of essential medicine in your purse.

☐ Don't wind your purse around your wrist. A purse snatcher will probably still be able to wrestle it away from you, and carrying it like this increases your chances of being injured as well as robbed.

❑ Keep your purse on your lap with your hands on it when you ride public transportation.

❑ When you go to the bathroom, keep your purse on your lap as much as possible.

❑ Carry a hardwood cane or an umbrella regardless of whether you need help in walking or in warding off showers. You can use either to defend yourself: smack your assailant's ankles or knees by swinging the cane or umbrella like a golf club. This is easier than swinging it like a baseball bat, and your assailant is less likely to grab your cane or umbrella away from you. You will also have better aim for vulnerable spots, such as the nose, eyes, or throat.

❑ Carry a noise alarm or police whistle.

❑ Avoid middle and junior high schools after school lets out.

❑ Avoid Laundromats and laundry rooms if you'll be there by yourself. Never go there alone at night. Always hold on to your purse or wallet regardless of what time you go.

❑ If you normally need glasses to dial the phone, check with your phone company to see if it has any aids to help you see your phone buttons. These can save you time, frustration, and anxiety in an emergency.

❑ If you are with a group of friends and are approached by hoods, form a circle and begin screaming.

To Prevent General Mistreatment

❑ Continue to be socially active. Keep in touch with old friends and make new ones.

❑ Participate in community activities.

❑ Have a buddy whom you see once a week outside your home.

❑ Keep regular appointments with your doctor, dentist, and hairdresser or barber.

❑ Ask friends to stop by and visit, even if you're living with someone else. It gives them a chance to check on how you're doing.

❑ Have your own telephone and open your own mail.

❑ Keep your belongings tidy and have a regular storage place for your personal belongings.

❑ Secure cash, jewelry, or treasured personal belongings.

❑ Keep control over your property and assets until you decide you can't manage them.

❑ Insist on having records, accounts, and property available for inspection by anyone you trust, not just the person you or the court has designated to manage your affairs.

❑ Don't trade care in return for transfer or assignment of your property or assets without a lawyer, advocate, or personal, trusted friend present to witness the transaction.

❑ Pay attention to the details of your personal affairs.

❑ Recognize that emotional abusiveness and intentional neglect often presage physical abuse. With that warning, you can act to change your living situation.

If Anything Happens

❑ Notify the police.

❑ Notify your insurance company if anything is stolen.

❑ If you were assaulted, check whether you're eligible for victim's compensation.

☐ If identification was stolen along with your keys, change your locks.

Getting older doesn't mean that you have to become fearful and a hermit. Actively working to stay safe means you can enjoy a busy, fulfilling life for years to come.

(See AT HOME, OUT AND ABOUT, STREET CRIME.)

6

CHILDREN

Peter was playing at the park by himself that afternoon. His friends had been called in for dinner, and he knew he probably should go home, too, but he wanted to finish carving one more road in the sand. He looked up when he heard a car stop close by. "Hello, young man," said a middle-aged, nicely dressed man. "Would you like to see the newest Nintendo game I have?" He held out a package toward Peter. Peter dropped his shovel and went toward the car . . . .

This scenario sends shivers down the spines of parents. We are more protective of our children than we are of ourselves. And we are continually reminded of terrible things that can happen to our innocent young ones. Stories of day care centers where children have been sexually abused generate community hysteria; articles about missing children haunt us as we send our own children off to play; a stream of reports about violence in schools nags us when we kiss our children good-bye in the morning as they pick up their backpacks and head off.

Part of protecting our children is teaching them to protect themselves. Vital to this process is keeping open lines of communication. To teach our children, we must talk to them in ways that they understand and take to heart. To learn of their problems and anything that might happen to them, they must be willing to talk to us, and we have to make the time and effort to understand what they're saying.

We parents have to base what we say on the age and maturity of the child and on his particular living and educational situation. A child attending a large, inner-city high school has different security worries than a child who goes to a small, rural elementary school.

Teach your child to comply with the safety precautions, including recommendations by the Child Safety Council. Do not scare your child into compliance unless absolutely necessary. The goal is to have your child act prudently without being unduly fearful. Use a matter-of-fact approach geared to the child's age and level of understanding. Often with young children their fear of being separated from their parents and their toys is enough to ensure compliance.

You do not need to be specific about the awful things that can happen to children if they go off with strangers. You do not need to tell them, for example, about ransoms, death, sexual assault. But you do need to get specific when discussing what children should and should not do. Telling them not to talk to strangers is plainly not enough.

When children ask why strangers do bad things to children, you can simply describe child molesters as "sick," rather than give graphic descriptions of sexual perversions. Stay away from abstract concepts such as guilt and sin.

And if the worst does happen, try to control your reaction in front of your child. Children often react in line with your reactions. If you are angry at the molester, a child will often interpret that as anger against himself, especially if the abuse happened because the child broke a safety rule. Even older children are often afraid of what will happen to them if they report the crime. You may also feel guilty that you were unable to protect your child. Bear this emotional burden by yourself, or share it with other adults when the child is not present. Instead, emphasize to the child that you are glad you know about what happened so that you can help and protect the child better.

The checklists in this chapter cover general guidelines that you should discuss with your child periodically. Some specific recommendations geared toward different age groups—preschoolers, early teens, older teens—follow. We include safety information on day care centers because this topic is such a huge worry for working parents; however, a child is more likely to be abused by an acquaintance at home than to be molested or harmed by a day care employee.

Concerns about how safe your child's school is, however, seem more warranted. Your child spends a large part of her day at school. Share with her the safety tips found here, but know the most important thing your child needs at school is credibility so that people will believe what she says. Teach your child to stand up for herself and to say "no" when it's appropriate.

If your child attends a large inner-city school, talk with school authorities for their recommendations on how to keep your child safe. The problems that beset such a school can be severe. Be aware, too, that the school is not responsible for anything that happens either off school grounds or before or after school, including weekends.

Teenagers are at most risk for many crimes. The Bureau of Justice Statistics concludes that

- Teenagers are more likely than adults to be assaulted during a crime, although they are less likely to be injured.

- Teenagers are more likely than adults to commit violent crimes against other teens.

- Boys in their teens actually have a higher chance of being victimized than teenage girls. Black teenage boys suffer the highest rate of victimization of all.

- Teens are usually preyed upon by people of their own racial background.

- Younger teens are likely to be robbed and assaulted on a street or in a park. At school or on school property they are often the victims of simple assault.

- Offenders are usually male, but one out of every sixteen male teens is the victim of female teenagers. And in one out of three cases, female teens face female offenders.

GENERAL GUIDELINES

Your children should know that unless they are with a parent, they should

☐ Never get into a car with a stranger. Explain that you would never send a stranger to pick them up.

☐ Never agree to help a stranger, even if he or she is upset. They should get a trusted adult to help the stranger.

☐ Never open the door if they don't recognize the voice of the person knocking.

☐ Always tell a parent, teacher, or neighbor right away if a stranger offers them candy, gifts, or a ride; tries to touch them; or makes them feel uncomfortable or funny.

☐ Never enter a stranger's house.

☐ Never let a stranger touch them or join in children's play.

☐ Never accept anything from a person they do not know.

☐ Always report any stranger who bothers them to parents, a teacher, law enforcement officer, bus driver, or an adult they know and can trust.

   - Always try to remember what the stranger looks like and how he is dressed.

- Always get the license number of his car. They can write it on a paper or on the sidewalk with a stone or scratch it in the dirt with a stick.

☐ Never go with any stranger who asks for directions.

☐ If they see a playmate get into a stranger's car, copy the license plate number and tell a parent, teacher, or police officer at once.

☐ Never tell strangers any personal information.

☐ Never go to playgrounds, movies, or other public places alone. Stay with friends.

☐ Never play alone in vacant buildings or alleys.

☐ When possible, travel to and from school with older children.

☐ Never go out alone after dark.

☐ Always go to a public rest room with an adult.

Other Precautions

☐ Read a book aloud on safety with your children. Try *Who Is a Stranger and What Should I Do?* by Linda Girard, or *Don't Touch Me There* by Oralee Wachter. Your librarian can make other recommendations.

☐ Help children figure out what to do by posing "what if" questions to them: "What would happen if . . . ?" "What can you do if . . . ?" "What else can you do?" Use role-playing so that the situations and their responses are more vivid to them.

☐ Let your children come up with suggestions first of what to do in a given situation.

☐ Keep asking questions so that children can come up with a variety of responses. This is especially important because not all dangerous people are strangers.

☐ Don't tell your children that only strangers can hurt them. In 60 percent of child molestation cases, the perpetrator is a relative, friend, or acquaintance of the child or his family.

☐ Teach your children the private parts of their bodies that only parents, doctors, or nurses should be allowed to touch. Use the words "We don't want *anyone* to touch you there," so that "anyone" doesn't refer only to strangers.

☐ Teach your children that good strangers leave children alone.

☐ Encourage children to trust their instincts.

☐ Trust your uneasy feelings about acquaintances or relatives who seem inordinately fond of little children.

☐ Give children examples of scary things that happened to you and what you did about it.

☐ Reassure your children that you won't get angry with them for telling you about someone who hurt them or made them feel funny or scared. Emphasize to your children that if they are molested, they should come tell you immediately and that it's not something they should feel bad about.

☐ Listen carefully to your children. Ask questions to help them be more specific, if necessary. Encourage your children to express their fears.

☐ Work with your Parent Teacher Association (PTA) to establish block programs for the neighborhood and ground rules for the schools.

☐ Try to walk with your children the first several days of school.

☐ Have your children walk on main streets, preferably busy ones, on their way to school. They should walk the same exact route every day.

☐ Teach your children to walk on the sidewalk facing traffic.

☐ At home put your children in bedrooms without an easy access from the outside. Have younger children leave their bedroom doors open at night so you can hear any disturbance.

☐ Teach children to keep the doors and windows locked and never to open the door to strangers, even if an adult is in the house. The child should call the adult to the door if a stranger is outside.

☐ Keep your children from being alone. Child molesters rarely approach groups of children.

☐ Never leave small children unattended even for a moment in your yard, car, shopping cart—anywhere.

☐ Follow the experts' advice: children should go to a woman, not a man, for help when faced with an emergency.

☐ Teach them which neighbors they can go to for assistance.

☐ Tell them to yell long and hard if someone comes after them.

☐ By age five children should know how to use the phone to call for help; they should also know their name, address, telephone number, where their parents work, and a work phone for their parents. Teach your children to dial "0" for an operator to help them get the police, the fire department, or an ambulance. They need to give their name, location, problem, and telephone number.

☐ Make sure they always have change to make a phone call.

☐ Consider enrolling your children in a martial arts course, to give them self-confidence rather than defense tools.

☐ Know where your children are at all times, who they are with, what they are doing, and when they are expected to return. This goes for teenagers as well as toddlers.

☐ Practice what you preach when it comes to safety habits. Lock your doors, watch what you tell strangers, and so forth.

☐ Teach your children to bring their possessions inside when they're through playing with them. Set a good example.

☐ Help them avoid drugs and alcohol.

☐ Get to know the parents of your children's friends. It's good to know if someone's folks are drug dealers, for example.

☐ If your political position or wealth makes your children an inviting target to kidnappers, explain to your children why you (and they) need to take extra precautions.

DAY CARE

☐ Be leery of a child care center that has restrictions on when you may visit.

☐ Choose child care that lets only authorized adults pick up your children at the end of the day.

☐ Ask the director how carefully she or he has checked the references and work histories of all the staff—the janitors, aides, and part-time help as well as the caregivers.

☐ Ask how the director handles behavior problems. Watch for signs of physical or other punishment.

☐ Ask the director about her or his feelings toward sexual abuse. Is she or he comfortable talking about it?

☐ Be wary of a closed bathroom door when an adult and a child are inside.

☐ In a child care center, there should be at least two adults in the room at any time to help stave off the possibility of one adult mistreating children.

☐ When you talk to your children about safety, don't link precautions to day care specifically. Simply give general rules.

☐ Don't grill your children about what goes on at day care in an effort to "communicate." You want your children to be receptive to normal affection and not to resist a caregiver who needs to help them use the bathroom or change their clothing.

☐ Always remind your children that you are in charge and that you are there to protect them from harm of any kind.

☐ Be suspicious of your child care situation if

- Your child displays distress persistently. Inexplicable crying, frequent nightmares, sudden changes in eating or sleeping habits, and firm resistance to going to the child care center are worth following up. And you should always ask about the circumstances leading to bruises or other injuries to your children.

- Your child becomes overly concerned about his or her genitals. Toilet talk is typical for young children, particularly around potty training time; but if your child is excessively focusing on his or her genitals, having nightmares or dreams about them, or being overly protective of them, you should talk to the caregiver right away.

- Your normally affectionate child shies away from cuddling.

☐ If you suspect abuse, visit the center, compare notes with other parents, and question the director and caregivers closely.

You should remember, however, that much more abuse takes place at home than at day care centers.

SCHOOL-AGED CHILDREN

☐ Visit your children's schools to see what security is in place. Do visitors have to report to the office? Are the grounds and halls supervised? Are playgrounds supervised after school hours, on weekends, and during vacation?

☐ Divorced parents: If you have sole custody of your children and believe your ex-spouse might try to kidnap them, take a picture of your ex to school (along with your divorce papers) and tell the school personnel to call the police if your ex shows up on the school grounds.

☐ Ascertain your school's policy about releasing children into the care of someone other than a parent.

☐ Urge your children not to risk their lives over a material possession—money, jacket, or shoes, for example. When outnumbered, they should give up the items and then work with authorities to rectify the situation.

☐ Discourage your children from boasting about or showing off any valuables or money they have on them.

☐ Tell your children to avoid gangs, kids crowding into one place, or any area where it looks like trouble is brewing. They should cross the street to avoid a group of trouble-makers or head into a business or store.

☐ Teach your children the same safety basics from other parts of this book. They include the following:

- If they encounter a burglar at home, they should get out of his way as fast as possible.
- If they suspect someone has broken into their home, they should not enter the house. Instead they should go to a phone and call the police and their parents.
- If they're in one part of the house and they hear a worrisome noise, they should turn on some lights and talk out loud as if they're talking to another person.

- If confronted by an armed robber, they should hand over whatever the thief wants. Nothing is worth getting killed over.
- If confronted by other kids who want to take something, the children should try to talk their way out of it. When push comes to shove, however, they should hand over what the kids want.
- Children should learn to carry their money in several places, just as adults should.

☐ Teach your children that policemen will help them. They should also learn who they can turn to in other situations. For example, in a museum they can go to a security guard; in a movie theater, an usher. Point these people out to your children as you happen to encounter them to prepare your children for any time they're out without you.

☐ If someone is following them, they should cross the street, change directions, vary their pace, run toward a safe place—someplace well lighted and busy.

☐ In dropping your children off at school or a friend's home, never leave until you're certain they are safely with others.

☐ When your child stays overnight with a friend, find an excuse to call and make sure he or she is there.

TEENAGERS

☐ Discuss rape with your daughter. Give her the following guidelines:

- Do not entertain male guests unsupervised.
- Teach her that saying, "No, I don't want to do that" is the best first approach to avoiding unwanted sexual activities. She doesn't have to say why. "No" is enough. If a young man doesn't stop his advances, a girl can leave him or go to a public place. Tell her that she can always call you for a ride.

- Dress appropriately.
- Travel in a group. There's safety in numbers.
- Be cautious when home alone during the day, such as after school.
- Stay away from isolated spots.

☐ Teach your teenagers that they should leave a party if guests are abusing alcohol or drugs. Emphasize that girls are more vulnerable to teenage boys who can become aggressive under the influence of alcohol or drugs.

☐ Ask baby-sitters to take the same precautions that you would in your own home—that is, locking the doors and windows, not giving out information about being alone over the phone, not opening the door to strangers, and so on.

☐ In their early teen years, encourage your children to be particularly cautious in public areas and report to the police any adult who loiters where teens usually congregate, who tries to approach them, who exposes himself, who offers them rides, and so forth.

☐ Make sure teenagers always travel with a companion.

☐ Discuss why they should not provoke trouble with their actions, speech, or dress.

☐ Never let them wander off into hidden and lonely spots where sex criminals like to lurk, such as lovers' lanes or any isolated parking spots.

☐ Tell the children that when they go to the movies, they should allow their eyes to adjust to the dark before picking a seat. Next to the aisle is best—you can move away quickly if annoyed.

☐ Never let them go alone to the beach or a park, especially after dark.

❏ Reassure them that regardless of the hour, place, or circumstances, you will always come and pick them up.

AT SCHOOL

It doesn't hurt to reiterate the following guidelines for your children during the school year.

❏ Don't take off jewelry when washing your hands in the bathroom.

❏ When changing clothes in the locker room, keep your wallet or purse in your locker, in your pocket, or close by and within sight.

❏ Don't leave your valuables in desks that don't lock or lockers that aren't secure.

❏ Especially girls, avoid being alone before or after school.

❏ In rougher schools, make sure you're not alone in a rest room, locker room, classroom, or corridor.

❏ Avoid kids you don't know when you're in public.

❏ Do your homework and chores after school and stay off the street.

❏ Ignore taunts that might provoke you into a fight. Fights tend to start in junior high (middle school); walk away from a fight. Encourage and congratulate your friends who also walk away from a fight.

❏ Your first measure of self-defense is to run.

❏ Your second line of defense is to yell "Fire."

❏ In dealing with gangs, your first approach is to try to avoid eye and body contact. The second is, if you have to talk to the gang, to make eye contact and appear strong and unafraid. Many factors are at play, however, when it comes to gangs, so it is difficult to make generalizations that will work every time.

☐ Know where hoods hang out, and avoid these areas.

☐ Sit with your friends as a protection against gangs.

☐ Bring only enough school supplies for yourself. And learn to say no to requests from thugs. "Will you lend me a pencil?" "No." "Can I have some paper?" "No." With such dead-end responses, a hood is less likely to press the relationship.

AS A PARENT

☐ Teach your children that standing up for themselves has consequences, but not defending themselves won't make them safe. Instead, they will be seen as weak and will be continually preyed upon.

☐ Participate in your children's school life: Go to open houses, stop by the school, and let your children's teacher(s) know who you are. Be nonadversarial if you need to discuss a child's performance with a teacher. In rougher schools, ask that teachers not send students into the halls alone, and give the children a time limit for returning.

☐ Support your school if the administration decides to pull out the lockers. Many of the problems with weapons and drugs at school disappear when lockers do.

☐ Emphasize to your children that they need to choose decent friends and say no to things that will get them in trouble.

☐ Discipline your child if he or she gets into trouble. Don't dismiss wrongdoing as nonconsequential. Studies have shown that if a child breaks rules and doesn't get caught, he'll do it again until he does get caught and his parents or guardians react in a big way. If he gets caught and isn't reprimanded, he'll do it again. Maybe he gets caught and maybe he doesn't. If he does, and nothing severe happens, it becomes a game for him. Will he get caught or won't he?

☐ If your child is harassed or assaulted by another child in class, send a note to the teacher insisting that the other child not be seated within 2 or 3 feet of your child. If the harassment or assaults continue and the school system won't take action (that is, the administration chooses not to expel the child), get a restraining order against the assailant. Name everyone in the child's household (including his parent's live-in boyfriend or girlfriend) in the order.

☐ Encourage your daughter to say "Don't talk to me like that" when boys make sexually abusive remarks. She shouldn't be aggressive, but matter-of-fact and consistent.

☐ Teach your children a few basic self-defense techniques to use if all else fails.

Self-Defense

☐ Kick the assailant's knee.

☐ Send a karate chop to the nose, under the nose, side of the neck, or to the shoulder muscle, bend of the elbow (to keep from being grabbed), mound of the forearm, abdomen, or knee. In a karate chop the thumb is held close to the hand, with the hand held stiffly and cupped slightly. Strike with the fleshy part of the side of the hand. When done correctly, there is no pain to the hand. Practice by hitting hard surfaces lightly.

☐ Squeeze and pull the attacker's testicles. This may not work, however, if the assailant is wearing jeans or another unyielding material.

☐ Press your thumbs into the attacker's eyes.

If Anything Happens

☐ If your worse fears about a day care center are confirmed, remove the child from the center immediately. Take your child for a complete medical checkup. Call the police. Contact other parents. Talk about the experience with your child: let the child know that what happened was not his or her fault and that you have rescued the child and will continue to protect him or her.

☐ If your child is molested,

- Make sure he or she receives professional counseling. Often the full impact of the incident doesn't hit until the child reaches puberty.
- Prosecute to the full extent possible, regardless of the age and sex of, or familial relationship with, the offender.
- Get as many details of the incident as possible.
- Respond in a way that's best for the child—one that protects the child and still satisfies justice.
- Report incidences.

☐ After an abuse has taken place, keep the child's routine as normal as possible. The hullabaloo about the abuse may cause more trauma and stress than the incident itself.

☐ If your child is abused, try to remain calm in the presence of the child. The child may misinterpret your emotions as being directed toward him or her.

☐ If kidnappers strike, don't panic. Call the police. Demand that the kidnappers put the child on the phone.

Teach, don't preach. Try to keep lines of communication open, and help your children to be confident and safe.

(See Street Crime.)

7

VEHICLE THEFT

CARS

He had the Jeep packed for his weekend in the mountains. He'd thought of everything . . . except that thermos of coffee he'd left on the kitchen counter. Leaving the car running, he headed back into the house. In the minute he was gone, three teenagers took the vehicle. Unfortunately for them, the owner of the Jeep was an off-duty police officer who immediately notified his office. Even more unfortunate, the high-speed chase that resulted left two of the boys critically injured and one permanently brain damaged after they lost control of the Jeep and smashed into a building.

We can learn two lessons here: even for those who know better it's easy to slip up; and any time a vehicle is stolen, it's usually returned damaged in some way—if the owner ever gets it back at all.

According to the FBI's *Uniform Crime Report*, every nineteen seconds in 1991, someone stole a motor vehicle. Eighty percent of those vehicles were passenger cars; 15 percent, trucks or buses;

and the remainder, "other" types that the FBI included in this category—motorcycles, motor scooters, snowmobiles, and so forth.
An estimated 1 of every 117 registered motor vehicles was stolen
nationwide during 1991. Regionally, the greatest risk of vehicle
theft is in the Northeast, where 1 of every 84 was stolen. The rates
for the other regions were 1 per 101 in the West, 1 per 127 in the
South, and 1 per 167 in the Midwest.

Offenders arrested were by and large young: 62 percent were
less than twenty-one years old, and 44 percent were younger than
eighteen. Ninety percent of those arrested were men; 59 percent
were white, and 39 percent were African American.

In the 1960s, nine out of every ten stolen cars were recovered,
abandoned by their teenage thieves after a joy ride. Today, only
about 60 percent of the owners will see their vehicles again.
Professionals who take cars for parts or resale have by-and-large
replaced the joy riders.

Who is most at risk? People who leave their keys in their cars.
People who don't lock their cars. And people who live in big cities.
In 1985, for example, a third of all auto thefts nationwide took
place in New York, Chicago, Los Angeles, Detroit, and Boston.

Some people mistakenly believe that only sports cars or very
expensive cars are stolen. In addition to being taken for parts,
"ordinary" cars are also stolen for use in other criminal activities,
such as bank robberies or drug dealing, or for part of an initiation
into a gang.

During 1991, the estimated value of motor vehicles stolen was
nearly $8.3 billion. But car theft costs are wide-ranging. First, even
if the car is covered by insurance, consider the victim's direct cost
of the car. Then there is the matter of time. Although a professional car thief can steal a car in less than a minute, it takes the victim
hours to fill out police and insurance reports and to recover or
replace the car. Police time and paperwork to investigate the crime
also run up the tab. As if that's not enough, every car stolen in
America contributes to the rising cost of insurance premiums for
all insured motorists. Besides the major inconvenience, all this

makes it well worth the effort to make sure your car isn't stolen in the first place.

The key to keeping your car safe is to remember that thieves want to do their work quickly and quietly. If you make it harder or more time consuming, odds are they'll move on to easier pickings.

The simplest precautions work best: Take your key out of the ignition. Roll up the windows. Lock your doors. In 1991, 40 percent of the cars stolen had a key in the ignition; 80 percent were unlocked.

You also have a variety of sirens and car alarms and other antitheft devices to choose from to impede a would-be car thief. In fact, it's a good idea to install several if you really want to stop a thief. A door alarm, for example, cuts off as soon as the thief can hop in your car and shut the door. So, having more than one antitheft device on your car makes sense. Be certain to check your local ordinances regarding car alarms first. Some are illegal in certain areas.

Some alarms go off if someone tries to grab parts of your car, such as your chrome wheels or your car stereo. Others blare when your car is moved to prevent it from being jacked up or towed away. All alarms use noise to startle a car thief away; cheapest are the ones that hook up to the car's horn. Most expensive and most effective are the alarms that sound like sirens.

You can install antitheft devices, either alone or in conjunction with alarms. Babaco alarms make sure the thief can't disconnect the sounding alarm. Another simple antitheft device is a steering wheel lock such as "The Club." Another is a gadget that causes a fuse to cut out after a minute or two if someone starts your vehicle after you have turned the system on.

You can also install an ignition-killer switch that makes it impossible for anyone to start your car unless he finds the switch first. Naturally you'd want to put the switch someplace tough to find—not the glove box.

There are even kits that offer a fake alarm switch and decal. These aren't going to fool the pros, but they'll ward off the inexperienced thief. Investigate the costs of antitheft devices and decide how much money and effort you want to spend on protecting your vehicle.

Anything you do to draw attention to a person trying to steal your car will deter the thief. Don't give the criminal a break. Another benefit to using antitheft devices is that many insurance companies offer discounts on premiums depending on the type of device installed, thus giving you a break.

Preventive Measures

☐ Take the key out of the ignition.

☐ Lock your car doors at all times and keep the windows rolled up.

☐ Park your car in a locked garage, if possible.

☐ Park in well-lighted, busy places if a locked garage is unavailable.

☐ If you have to use a parking lot, use one that will let you lock your car and take your keys with you.

☐ In parking lots where you must leave your key, give the attendant only your car key, not your whole key chain. You don't want to give the attendant the opportunity to copy your house key.

☐ In parking garages, park your car close to the street, close to the attendant's booth, or in the best-lighted, busiest area you can find.

☐ Turn your wheels sharply to the right or left. This deters professional thieves who prefer to tow cars away.

☐ Don't hide a spare key in your car. Odds are a thief will think of the same hiding place.

❏ Install antitheft devices and alarms—and remember to turn them on, if they don't come on automatically, when you get out of the car. Avoid depending solely on factory-installed alarms; thieves can easily determine how to disconnect these standard systems. And check to see if any are illegal where you live.

❏ You can use devices to lock up your steering column, but be aware that thieves keep up with technology. Liquid nitrogen is being used to cut through "The Club" on your wheel.

❏ Replace your door lock buttons, if necessary, with slim, tapered ones that can't be pulled up by an untwisted coat hanger.

❏ Remove a small but essential part of the engine, such as the distributor rotor (your mechanic can show you how). This is more practical when you are going to be leaving your car in one spot for a while than if you are going in and out on errands, but it is simple and effective.

❏ Consider using a hardened-steel chain and a case-hardened padlock to fasten your car hood to the grill.

❏ Carry your registration with you, rather than leave it in the car. If the driver of a stolen car is stopped for some reason and can't produce the registration, the police officer routinely checks the status of the car. This means the thief gets apprehended and your car is returned to you.

❏ Scribble a note on the back of an envelope saying "Gone for gas," "Sugar in tank," or "Motor dead" to put under the windshield wiper when you leave the car. While it looks like a message to ticket writers or police, literate thieves will probably pass up a car that looks as if it won't run.

❏ To make it easier to recover your vehicle if it is stolen, etch the vehicle identification numbers on some obscure part of the car's chassis. In the same spirit, you can drop your business card inside the door panels.

☐ Don't leave anything with your address in your car. That includes mail and magazines with subscription labels on them. The thief may begin with larceny—stealing your car—and end up committing burglary by stealing from your home.

☐ Don't leave your car unattended for long periods of time, like in an airport long-term parking lot. Have someone drive you, or take public transportation or a cab.

☐ If you do leave your car in the airport or train depot parking lot, take the parking voucher with you.

☐ If your car breaks down, try to stay with it till help arrives. Auto thieves can use a tow truck to take away temporarily abandoned cars.

☐ When selling your car, don't allow someone to take your vehicle out for a test-drive without taking something valuable, such as a credit card, as security. Don't go along. Going for a test-drive with a stranger leaves you vulnerable to assault or rape.

☐ Don't pick up hitchhikers.

Carjacking

By and large auto theft is committed without the car owner seeing the perpetrator. When a thief carjacks your vehicle, he takes it from you personally, often threatening you with a gun or knife.

Carjackings made up less than 2 percent of all auto thefts in 1991, but police in major metropolitan areas and their suburbs have seen a recent rise in this method of stealing, possibly because more sophisticated alarms are making it difficult for thieves to steal cars.

The least that can happen in a carjacking is you lose your car. And the good news is that 90 percent of carjacked vehicles are recovered relatively quickly. But, as in many confrontations with an armed criminal who wants your possessions, carjackings can turn deadly. Such was the case when two men in a Washington, D.C., suburb took a BMW from a woman driving her child to preschool. Entering the car while the driver was stopped at an intersection, they shoved her out, but one of her arms got tangled in a safety belt. She died after she was dragged a mile and a half. The child was later found unharmed in her safety seat along the side of the road.

In response to such cases, federal legislators passed a law in October 1992 making it a federal crime to use a gun in auto theft. Conviction carries a minimum sentence of fifteen years.

A Maryland State Police report analyzed 445 carjacking incidents in the Baltimore area during 1992. According to the report, carjackers are not selective about their targets—either the driver or the car. This report supports the idea that carjacking is a "crime of opportunity." You want to make sure you don't present an opportunity!

The Maryland police report offered these other interesting statistics:

About 51 percent of all carjackings occurred while the cars were parked.

Carjackings took place most often (14.4 percent) at apartments, followed by on the open road (13.8 percent); at shopping centers (12.8 percent); at gasoline stations (10.3 percent); in residential driveways (4.2 percent); and in public parking lots or garages (less than 4 percent).

Approximately 67 percent of the reported carjacking victims were male, and 68 percent were African American. About 40 percent were between the ages of 21 and 30; 12.7 percent were 50 or older.

More Chevrolets (17 percent) were carjacked than any other car, followed by Nissans (13 percent).

To thwart would-be carjackers, in addition to the general advice to avoid having your car stolen, take the following precautions.

Preventive Measures

☐ Be aware of your surroundings and people in the area. Look to see what any people nearby are doing as you approach and enter your car. As you sit in traffic, pay attention so you can see anyone approaching your car.

☐ Keep your car doors locked and the windows up. If you don't have air conditioning, crack the window a bit, but not enough to let in someone's arm.

☐ Keep your valuables out of sight. Put them in the glove box or the trunk or under your seat. Why add incentives to stealing your car?

☐ If you are stopped at a red light and someone tries to get in, honk your horn repeatedly to try to scare the thief off, and drive off, even if you risk a collision. Turning to the right—which will put you going in the same direction as the nearest moving traffic—minimizes the danger of a collision. And if you do have an accident, stay in your car and drive to a service station to use the phone. This doesn't count as leaving the scene of an accident, since you are merely going to the nearest phone to report it.

☐ Keep your car in good working condition, with plenty of gas, so your car won't fail during critical moments.

☐ Travel with a companion when possible. Carjackings usually involve a lone person in the car.

☐ Don't fall for the "bump and rob" method. Carjackers sometimes roll up behind potential victims and bump them. When the victim gets out to inspect the damage, the car is stolen. Unless others are around, don't get out of your car. Instead, drive to a phone to report the incident, or motion the other car to follow you while you drive to find a police station or a police officer.

❑ Use well-lighted routes when possible.

❑ Drive in the center lane on city streets.

❑ Keep your car keys separate from house keys. This ensures that if your car does get taken, you don't have to worry about the security of your home as well.

❑ When returning home, try to have someone turn the lights on or greet you at the door.

Car Stripping

Having parts stolen from your car, while not as shocking as having your entire vehicle stolen, is irritating and inconvenient. It may be the battery, the windshield wipers, or custom wheels, covers, and tires. Regardless of the part or the expense, it still offends your sense of privacy and decency.

The thieves who swipe car parts off the street tend to be "local yokels" up to no good; professionals prefer to steal the car and take it to a "chop shop," where the entire car is cut into resalable parts.

Cars that make more attractive targets are usually

- less than two years old or are in exceptionally good shape;
- parked on the street or on an unattended lot;
- parked on a side street or on a poorly lit street;
- left overnight or over the weekend for service somewhere;
- rare models, popular classics, or a collector's item;
- fitted with custom wheel covers, wheels, or tires; or
- equipped with tempting electronics.

Thefts of motor vehicle parts, accessories, and contents made up the largest portion of larcenies reported to the FBI, or 37 percent.

Preventive Measures

- [ ] Lock your car.
- [ ] Reinforce the trunk lock with a heavy-duty plate and lock assembly.
- [ ] Install a hood lock if you don't have one already.
- [ ] Invest in a car alarm, including a motion-sensitive alarm that goes off if the vehicle is jacked or moved.
- [ ] Put valuables—and containers, such as suitcases, that might hold valuables—out of sight, preferably in your trunk.
- [ ] Or take valuables with you. Stereos and CB radios can be installed on a two-piece mounting bracket. One part stays in your car; the other part, which has the stereo mounted to it, you slide out when you leave the car and click easily back in place when you return.
- [ ] Inscribe the vehicle identification number on a couple of places in your car, such as the windows, both to deter someone from taking it and to make recovery possible.
- [ ] Buy and use lockable wheel covers or locking stud nuts.
- [ ] If you don't have a garage space with a lock, consider renting one.
- [ ] Park in a well-lit, busy street where a thief stripping your car—or your car alarm—would be more likely to attract attention.
- [ ] Lock your battery in place with a special clamping device.
- [ ] Use a "quick-disconnect" antenna attachment that lets you remove the antenna when you leave.

❏ Remove manufacturers' decals advertising expensive car parts.

(See OUT AND ABOUT: IN YOUR CAR, PARKING LOTS.*)*

BICYCLES

Janice B., a seventh-grader, left her new birthday bicycle in the school's bike rack at the beginning of the day. Because she was running late, she didn't bother to lock it up. When school let out, she came out to find her prized bike gone.

Most bike thieves don't need all the time a school day offers to swipe a bike. In a police experiment, unlocked bikes put in downtown Oakland, California, lasted an average of twenty seconds before being stolen.

As with most thefts, prevention is the precaution. Choosing the right padlock and chain or cable, remembering to use them, and avoiding high-crime areas are among the simple measures you can take to protect your bicycle.

Preventive Measures

❏ Keep your bicycle inside a locked garage or home when you're not using it.

❏ Always lock your bicycle.

❏ Choose a good padlock.

❏ Make sure your padlock is case-hardened steel with a shackle of at least 9/32 inches with a double-locking mechanism in both the heel and toes, a five-pin tumbler, and a key-retaining feature that keeps the key in the lock until the padlock is fully engaged.

❏ If you use a cable, thread it through the bike's frame, seat, handlebars, and both wheels.

☐ If you buy a special bicycle lock, be prepared to take the bike's front wheel with you whenever you leave your bike, or buy an extra length of cable to attach the front wheel to the frame.

☐ Buy at least a 5/16-inch chain of hardened steel alloy with a link of continuous construction.

☐ If you use a chain, secure both front and back wheels and the frame to a solid object with it.

☐ Keep the chain or cable as high off the ground as possible. Otherwise the thief can use the ground as an anvil to smash the chain against with a hammer or as leverage for a pry bar or bolt cutter.

☐ Fasten your bike next to a solid object, not to something that can be cut easily. Pick an object that can't be moved and that is very tall. Your bicycle and its chain can be lifted over the top of a parking meter; it can't be lifted off a telephone pole.

☐ Park your bike where other bikes are parked. This discourages a thief because he never knows when one of the owners might be returning.

☐ Register your bicycle with local police. Inscribe the registration number in several places on the bicycle's frame to help you get your bike back if it does get stolen.

MOTORCYCLES

In 1991, in California alone, 14,183 motorcycles were stolen. Motorcycles are a popular item with thieves for two simple reasons: they're easy to steal because their integral ignition-switch locks are relatively weak; and it's difficult to trace stolen motorcycle parts. As with automobiles and trucks, motorcycle thieves are more often professionals looking for a motorcycle they can steal for parts than teens out for kicks. But you can take the following steps to keep your motorbike safe.

Preventive Measures

☐ Turn your key to "Lock" every time you shut off your motorcycle.

☐ Store it in a locked garage, or at least under an unadorned motorcycle cover, and choose parking spots where a thief is likely to be noticed.

☐ Invest in an additional lock that will secure the frame or lock one of the motorcycle's wheels to an immovable object. If you can't attach the lock to a signpost, for example, at least put it on your front wheel. A simple padlock through the brake disc can also impede a thief. Just remember to remove it before driving off!

☐ Consider installing an alarm system. If you don't want to go to that extent, fake alarms are available that either blink or beep to make observers think the bike is armed.

☐ If you choose a real alarm system, be mindful of how much power the system uses. Some systems can sap a motorcycle's battery in days.

☐ If you put in an alarm system, remember to switch it on consistently.

☐ Make a habit of flicking off the engine "kill" switch when you park. Unobservant thieves have been known to give up on bikes that didn't start immediately.

☐ Remove the ignition fuse.

☐ When you sell your bike, do not allow test rides.

BOATS

Boat theft is a lucrative illegal business. Thousands of private and commercial boats are stolen each year. And as with cars, parts may be stolen instead of the entire vehicle. Engines and instruments are among the expensive pieces that a thief may pluck from a boat.

Stealing a boat is relatively simple, even in broad daylight. All a person has to do is back his vehicle up to a boat mounted on a trailer, hook it up, and drive away.

If a good-sized boat is in a marina, you should add locks and alarms to the doors and windows just as you would to your home or car. Shop for the system that suits your situation the best—whether it's an alarm that's hooked up to the boat's horn or a loudspeaker that identifies which boat in the marina contains an intruder.

Preventive Measures

☐ Never leave your boat's ignition key in the boat.

☐ Buy a locking cover for the trailer hitch if your boat is mounted on a trailer. When you park the boat for long periods, remove a wheel from the trailer.

☐ Remove the boat's battery if you won't be using the craft for a long time.

☐ Report suspicious individuals around your boat or the marina to the police and to the proprietors.

☐ To help recover your boat or parts if stolen, keep up-to-date photographs of your boat and equipment, and maintain a complete inventory of equipment and a detailed listing of serial numbers and hull identification numbers. Affix a personal identification code in secret locations. Otherwise, the police have very little to go on in recovering your property.

AIRPLANES

Stealing aircraft requires more sophistication than stealing a car or boat, but it happens. Some aircraft are stolen for use in illegal drug trafficking. Most are flown out of the state where they are stolen and never recovered. As with other vehicles, airplane equipment and instruments can easily be stripped and resold. To keep your craft safe and whole, observe the following precautions.

Preventive Measures

☐ Lock your airplane. It is not too big to be stolen.

☐ Store your aircraft inside a secure hangar. Try to use hangars or a well-locked private field, not an isolated, deserted field.

☐ Insist that the hangar be well lighted.

☐ If your aircraft is parked outside, lock the doors and chock the wheels. Use metal tie-down cable that will resist cutting.

☐ Always take the ignition key out of the aircraft. If you have to leave an extra key with airport personnel, ask them to explain their key-control procedures to you.

☐ Never leave valuable items inside the aircraft.

☐ Install an alarm system and antitheft devices.

☐ Check on the airport's security periodically.

☐ Do not store the aircraft log book with the aircraft.

☐ Do not take on passengers who request flights across borders or into secluded locations. This is a sign of possible drug or illegal alien smuggling.

☐ Maintain a record of aircraft serial numbers, including the engine identification number and the serial numbers on such equipment as radios and navigational aids. Also keep a current photograph of your plane to help police in recovering your property if it does get stolen.

If Your Vehicle, Boat, or Aircraft Is Stolen

❑ Report it to the local police.

❑ Report it to security at the garage, marina, or hangar, if your vehicle was stored there.

❑ Notify your insurance company.

❑ If your boat is stolen, also notify the state police, the U.S. Coast Guard, and the dealer where you bought the boat.

If a thief really wants your vehicle, boat, or aircraft, there are ways for him to take it. But most thieves want to snatch their target quickly and easily. By taking the measures discussed above, you encourage them to look for easier pickings.

8

TRAVEL

In the movie *Home Alone,* the young hero dissuades burglars from entering his home one evening by having what looked from the outside like a party. Little did the bad guys know that the "guests" were actually cutouts animated by wires. As with everyday home security, making your home look as if someone is there is your primary objective when you are preparing to leave on vacation.

And almost regardless of where you go, whether you're off camping or on a tour of the Continent, you'll be vulnerable to street crime and assault.

(See STREET CRIME: RAPE; VEHICLE THEFT.)

BEFORE YOU GO

Preventive Measures

❑ Discontinue regular deliveries, like the mail and newspaper. Better yet, have someone you trust pick up the mail and paper every day. Newspaper and mail carriers occasionally commit burglaries or theft, or tell someone else about a good opportunity to do so.

❏ Don't temporarily disconnect your telephone.

❏ If you know your destination, use call forwarding to forward calls from your home number to the number where you're staying while on vacation.

❏ Use a timer or photosensitive switch to turn one or more lights on and off. You can set several timers so that, for example, when the light goes off in the living room another comes on in the bedroom, to give the impression that you are moving throughout the house. You don't want to leave the living room lights on all night—a tip-off that no one's home. Hours without a shadow on the blinds sends the "all-clear" signal to a burglar, too.

❏ Attach a timer to your radio, set to a talk station with the volume low. This gives the impression that people are talking inside the home.

❏ Go outside at night and determine where you can see in, then go inside and make adjustments to your draperies and blinds.

❏ Arrange for someone to come change the position of your blinds and draperies every day or so.

❏ Arrange to have your lawn mowed and watered. In the winter, have someone shovel the snow off your walk, drive up and down your driveway, and leave footprints in the snow around your house.

❏ Ask your neighbors to keep an eye on your place while you're gone.

❏ If your trip will be a long one, let the police know how long you will be gone, who has a key to your house, and where you can be reached.

❑ Put your valuables in a safe-deposit box or vault. Deposit any extra cash into the bank as well.

❑ If you have more than one car, lend one to a friend or ask a neighbor to move one every day or so.

❑ Ask a neighbor to park in your drive.

❑ Always put all ladders, tools, lawn furniture, garbage cans, and so forth into a shed, garage, or basement.

❑ Make sure all the doors and windows are locked.

❑ If you are leaving a vehicle in your driveway, make sure it is locked.

❑ Close and lock your garage door.

❑ If you have a sliding glass door, drill a downward-sloping hole through the top channel into the top part of the door frame, then put in a quarter-inch pin or heavy nail through the frame and into the door. Use this security measure along with the other locks on your sliding doors.

❑ Set your air conditioner to "circulate" rather than turning it off when you are gone during hot summer months; an idle air conditioner is a dead giveaway that no one's home. Putting it on circulate saves energy but makes as much noise as when the air conditioner is set to "cool."

❑ If you are still worried about someone breaking in while you're on vacation, hire a security service. A private security agency can stand guard outside your home on a full- or part-time basis or include your home on regular security rounds. The cost depends on the degree of security you want.

❑ Don't let any notice of your trip run in the paper before you go. Tell your story when you get back.

❏ Tell casual acquaintances—your barber, auto mechanic, TV repairman—about your trip after you come back, not before.

❏ Sublet at a nominal fee or get a house-sitter.

❏ Scatter children's toys around the yard.

❏ Leave an itinerary with someone that lists the hotels and phone numbers where you can be reached, especially if you're traveling alone.

❏ Don't take a great deal of cash with you—and divvy that up among your purse, wallet, and pockets. Don't carry more than you can afford to lose.

❏ Take as little luggage as possible. Ideally, all you'd have is a carry-on bag.

❏ Avoid soft-sided luggage, which can easily be slashed.

❏ Leave anything home you would hate to lose, such as family objects, extra credit cards, or expensive jewelry.

❏ For a car trip, secure luggage on top of your vehicle with strong fasteners and good locks.

❏ Buy a CB and a good antenna.

❏ Plan your route carefully.

❏ If you're going hunting, unload your guns and lock them away any time you're not using them. Keep the ammunition separate from the guns.

WHILE YOU'RE ON VACATION

❏ Avoid telling strangers what hotel you're staying in.

❏ Compare the taxi driver's face with his ID before you shut the door. If they don't match, take a different taxi.

☐ Don't wear jewelry and keep watches out of sight. If you need to wear jewelry for a special occasion, keep it under your coat until you have arrived.

☐ Also keep your money concealed.

☐ Avoid street vendors and crowds, where pickpockets work.

☐ Know where you are going before you leave your accommodations. Ask directions and carry a street map with you.

☐ Walk swiftly and as if you know where you're going.

☐ If you've gone shopping and your arms are full, don't walk back to where you are staying. Take a taxi.

AT THE AIRPORT

Your Luggage

☐ Don't overstuff your luggage. These bags are more prone to open when dropped, allowing someone to help themselves to your property.

☐ Don't put your home address on the ID tag on your luggage. Put your name and a business address or the address of your hotel.

☐ Put your name and destination on a card inside each of your bags.

☐ Mark everything you carry in some distinctive way so you can recognize them even at a distance as yours. A piece of ribbon tied or stitched on or colored tape works well.

☐ Wrap a dozen loops of string around your suitcase in both directions. Doing so encourages dishonest baggage handlers to find easier bags to open.

❏ Drop your luggage off at the terminal at the curbside check-in or with a skycap before you find a parking place. You can move faster through the parking lot, where muggers might lurk, without your luggage.

❏ Check your luggage at the baggage counter instead of using any of the lockers in terminals.

❏ Make sure you receive a claim check for each piece of luggage you check.

❏ If you do use a locker and someone helps you load your luggage into it, make sure right then that the key your benefactor hands you actually opens the locker. Some con artists switch keys, letting them make off with your luggage before you come back to find your key doesn't open the locker.

❏ If someone picks up your luggage and starts to leave, yell "Hey there" loudly and indignantly. Odds are the would-be thief will drop your luggage and run or pretend it was a mistake and apologize.

❏ Make your own luggage your first priority. Don't be taken in by sets of thieves who ask you to watch a piece of luggage, lure you into giving chase when that luggage is swiped, and steal your luggage while you're pursuing the thief's luggage.

❏ Keep your luggage between your legs when it's not in your hand to prevent thieves from lifting it with their own "trapdoor" suitcase—a false-bottom suitcase that grips your suitcase as the thief lifts it and walks away.

❏ Pay particular attention to your belongings as they go through the security counter. Don't let any disturbances distract you, or your possessions may not be waiting for you when you clear security.

Public Bathrooms

☐ Try to leave your luggage with someone you know when you go to the rest room so you have less to keep track of. As an alternative, store it in a security locker. Failing that, make sure you keep an eye, if not a hand, on it at all times.

☐ In a public bathroom, don't take off your jewelry before washing your hands and face.

☐ If your small children need to go to the bathroom, go with them. If you need to go to the bathroom, bring them with you.

Parking Lots

☐ Have a cab take you to your car in the lot, especially if it's at night and you're by yourself. And give the driver an extra tip to see you safely to the exit.

☐ Before you park in the airport parking lot, look around to see if anyone is loitering around the cars. Airports are places where people should be hurrying to get to or from someplace; idlers are suspicious. If you see any, go to the cashier at the exit and request that security investigate.

Cabs

☐ Decline solicitations from cabbies who have a friend in the front seat. You don't want to be in a two-against-one situation.

☐ If your bus or train takes you to an undesirable section of town that you don't know, call a cab to take you to your final destination. The fare isn't too much to pay for keeping your valuables, luggage, and yourself safe.

☐ Be leery of people who suggest sharing a taxi into town, unless you saw the people on your flight.

☐ Don't sleep aboard trains, planes, or buses without making sure your valuables are as secure and unavailable as possible.

☐ Try to figure out cab fares before you actually get in a taxi, particularly where there's likely to be a language barrier. You don't want to pay $175 for a $25 trip.

Other Preventive Measures

☐ In a largely deserted airport, be especially alert in rest rooms, at food-service areas, and on boarding platforms.

☐ Avoid sections where there are boisterous teenagers.

☐ Never give your name and hotel address to strangers for any reason.

☐ Keep your ticket safe until you actually board. Don't fall for someone in uniform exchanging tickets for what turn out to be phony boarding passes.

☐ Use a money belt or a fanny pack.

☐ Make a list of serial and identification numbers of the valuables you're taking on your trip and put it with the list of traveler's check numbers in a safe place separate from your valuables and checks.

IN HOTELS

Choosing a Hotel

☐ Pick a hotel in a good neighborhood. When you're planning your trip, you can call the local police in the city where you're going and ask if a hotel you're considering is in a neighborhood you should avoid. If the officer is reluctant to answer for the department, ask if he would want his own family staying there.

☐ Pick a hotel in which rooms are accessed from an interior hallway. Motels and hotels with rooms that are accessed from the outdoors offer less security.

☐ It's better to pick a hotel where you'll be able to see your car from your room.

☐ Book a room that is between the second and seventh floors. This prevents easy access but is low enough for fire equipment to reach.

Registering

☐ If you're a woman traveling alone, register with an initial and your last name without using Ms. or Mrs.

☐ Don't say your room number out loud when you get your key; if the person at registration does, ask for a different room.

☐ Have the bellhop accompany you to your room and make sure no one is in it. Before he leaves, check that your phone is working and that emergency numbers are by the phone.

☐ If you think someone is following you when you leave the registration area, go to a hotel phone and pretend to be dialing. The impression that you're calling someone in the hotel to come meet you should get rid of the problem.

☐ If someone does follow you to your room, go past your room, down the hall, turn around, and go back to the elevator. Or knock on the door of your room as if someone is there already. Or if the person is persistent, use a hotel phone to call security for help.

Locks

☐ Use a travel lock to secure valuables in the top drawer of the dresser. Hook the lock over the other lip of the drawer and lock it. Use only the top drawer; other drawers can be accessed by pulling out the drawer above them.

☐ Carry a portable travel lock and a travel alarm for doors and windows.

☐ Use a travel lock on your sliding glass doors and windows in your hotel room.

☐ Use a bicycle lock and chain to attach your suitcases to radiator or bathroom pipes in your hotel room.

☐ Wedge a chair back under the doorknob. This really is an effective deterrent to opening the door, not just a joke from the movies. A rubber doorstop also works well.

☐ Make sure the hotel you choose has double locks on the door and that the locks work. If the locks are broken, ask for a different room.

☐ Lock your door and chain it as soon as you enter the room.

☐ Always keep your doors and windows locked.

☐ Before you go to sleep, balance an empty dresser drawer on the door molding—the part of the door frame that sticks out—or on the doorknob. It will fall off and wake you up if someone tries to come in that way.

Going Out

☐ Leave at least one light on when you leave the room. If you come back to a dark room, head for the lobby—without going in—and tell the people at the front desk.

❏ Ask the desk clerk or call local police to find out which areas to avoid traveling in.

❏ When you rent a car, get clear directions from the rental car agency to your hotel.

❏ Avoid being alone. Go out with a group, if possible, especially at night.

❏ Never keep expensive jewelry in your hotel room. Always put it in the hotel safe if you're not wearing it.

❏ Keep your wallet, traveler's checks, and passport out of sight.

❏ Don't leave your keys in your room.

❏ Visit intriguing, out-of-the-way spots during the day.

❏ Rig up an intrusion detector. Stick one end of a thin strip of gum or a thread to the door frame, the other to the door. If the strand is broken when you get back, get security to check out the room before you enter.

❏ When you come back after dark, use the main entrance.

❏ Check at the front desk to see if the hotel has a "return to room" escort service.

❏ When you come back to a hotel room, check in likely hiding spots. If you find someone, scream "Fire," and run.

Other Preventive Measures

❏ Remember to turn your car alarm on when you park at a hotel.

❏ Don't leave luggage in the car, even for one night.

❏ Be alert when going to the ice and vending machines; they're usually in isolated spots. Don't leave your door ajar when you make a trip to the machines.

❑ Be most alert in the hallways and parking areas.

❑ If someone knocks on your door, make sure it is room service before you open up. Don't open the door to any stranger you're not expecting. Call the front desk to determine the credibility of anyone who says he is from the hotel staff.

❑ Check your belongings into the hotel's checkroom if you're going to go sight-seeing that last day after checking out. It's safer than loading all your belongings into the car.

WHILE CAMPING

Preventive Measures

❑ If you have an alarm system in your car, wire your camper as well.

❑ Invest in a lock that fits over the trailer hitch when your camper is unhooked.

❑ Bring along a chest that you can lock your supplies in while you're off exploring nature.

❑ Check in with ranger stations or park police to find out which camping sites they suggest and to let them know you're around.

❑ Lock camper or motor home doors and windows, even when driving.

❑ For camping trips, take the junky stuff—stuff that's less likely to be attractive to thieves, like the beat-up radio instead of the expensive portable CD player.

❑ Park your motor home in areas designated for recreational vehicles, not in a campground, along the road, or in a deserted area.

IN FOREIGN COUNTRIES

Before You Go

☐ Learn enough of the language to ask for help, to report a crime, and to ask if English is spoken.

☐ Stay abreast of the news to be aware of any potential problems. Your alertness and the precautions you take should increase if you travel in areas where the potential for violence or terrorism is greater. Before going into troubled areas, you can check with the nearest U.S. Embassy or consulate regarding any adverse conditions you should be aware of. Ask for the American Citizens Service Unit in the consular section. To hear State Department travel advisories on a recording, call 202-647-5225 anytime.

☐ Use AAA, travel agencies, or other reliable sources, rather than strangers, for recommendations about where to visit.

☐ Use a travel agency with a twenty-four-hour phone link so you can make changes in your itinerary during off hours, if necessary.

☐ Carry traveler's checks instead of cash. Only sign traveler's checks in front of the person who will cash them, and be sure your credit card is returned to you after each transaction.

☐ Put the registration numbers of your traveler's checks in a different place than the checks themselves. If the checks get stolen, you'll need the numbers to have them replaced.

☐ Wrapping rubber bands around your wallet or keeping it in a zipped portion of a handbag makes it more difficult for a pickpocket to remove.

When You Arrive

☐ If possible, book a room between the second and seventh floors—above ground level to prevent easy entrance from the outside but low enough for fire equipment to reach.

☐ Make a note of emergency numbers: police, fire, your hotel, the nearest U.S. Embassy or consulate. Know how to use a pay phone and have the proper change or token on hand.

☐ Figure out which uniform the police wear so you can identify whom to run to in an emergency.

☐ Keep hotel and car keys on your person.

☐ If any of your possessions are lost or stolen, report the loss immediately to the police and other appropriate authorities. Keep a copy of the police report for insurance claims and as an explanation of your situation. Report the loss of traveler's checks to the nearest office of the issuing company or its agent; airline tickets, to the airline company or travel agent; and your passport, to the nearest U.S. Embassy or consulate.

☐ Carry a valid copy of your birth certificate. If your passport does get stolen, this makes it easier to get a new one while you're abroad.

☐ Keep a low profile. Dress and behave conservatively, avoiding flashy dress, jewelry, luggage, rental cars, or conspicuous behavior that would draw attention to you as a potentially wealthy or important foreigner.

☐ Be polite and low key. Avoid loud conversations and arguments.

☐ Let someone know when you expect to return, especially if you expect to be out late at night.

❏ Don't give your room number to anyone you don't know well. Meet visitors in the lobby.

❏ Avoid dangerous areas; don't use shortcuts, narrow alleys, or poorly lit streets. Try not to travel alone at night.

❏ Be alert to street gangs in large cities.

❏ Don't fight attackers. Give up your valuables.

When Driving

❏ Drive the more common kinds of locally available cars; if there aren't many American cars in use, don't insist on an American model.

❏ Make sure the car is in good repair.

❏ Keep car doors locked all the time.

❏ Don't park on the street overnight if the hotel has a garage or secure area. If you must park on the street, choose a well-lit area. Don't leave valuables in the car.

❏ Never pick up hitchhikers.

❏ Don't get out of the car if there are suspicious-looking people near. Drive away.

❏ Carry a flashlight in case of road emergencies.

(See TRAVEL: IN HOTELS; TERRORISM.)

ON BUSINESS TRIPS

Preventive Measures

☐ Give yourself plenty of time to get to where you're going. Haste leads to carelessness and preoccupation with your destination. You must be alert to avoid being victimized.

☐ Don't get careless with your possessions. Know where they are at all times; preferably hold on to them at all times.

☐ Don't drink heavily, either the night before you leave or while you're on your trip. You want to be alert, especially in unfamiliar places.

☐ Keep all the locks on your hotel room locked while you're in the room.

☐ Put a rubber doorstop under the door for extra security.

☐ Consider putting a portable door alarm on the door as well.

☐ Don't draw attention to yourself.

☐ Avoid arguments with service people, such as waiters, people setting up your business exhibit, bartenders, and so forth. They may react in dangerous ways you don't expect.

☐ When you're unwinding with your business associates at the end of the day, don't move the party to your room if you don't know all the people attending.

☐ Avoid pairs of prostitutes. One can keep you busy while the other is busy stealing all your valuables.

☐ Don't reveal personal information to people you've just met that would give them the idea that you have something worth stealing or that you're worth kidnapping.

OVERSEAS BUSINESS TRIPS

Preventive Measures

☐ Study. Bone up with maps. Learn about the culture and any current unrest. Forewarned is forearmed.

☐ Have someone familiar with the local area make your reservations and find a driver and translator. Stick with their recommendations on hotels and travel routes.

☐ Keep a low profile.

☐ Vary your route.

☐ Don't debate with strangers.

☐ Take taxis and guided tours.

☐ Always lock your car, regardless of how briefly you'll be away from it.

☐ Beware of phony road crews. If people dressed as public utility crews or road repair workers try to slow you down or stop you, look to make sure they have the normal equipment and attire and look for evidence of work.

☐ Avoid taking your road map into restaurants to peruse. Doing so would flag you as someone unfamiliar with the area.

☐ Always carry a flashlight in case of road emergencies.

When you travel, whether it's for business or pleasure, you don't want it marred by crime. And you don't want to spend precious time filling out police reports, in any language. Be alert, be prepared, and play it safe.

9

TERRORISM

A terrorist attack is by definition a random and unpredictable act. Americans used to think of terrorism as happening only in other countries, but the bombing of the World Trade Center in New York City in 1993 reminded us all too vividly that violent people with a cause can operate inside the United States as well. From 1987 through 1991, for example, there were thirty-four terrorist incidents in the United States and Puerto Rico. The advice we give in this chapter is written for those traveling abroad, but it can apply to those traveling in the United States as well.

When you are traveling in foreign countries, the best way to guard against becoming the victim of a terrorist act is to avoid areas where there has been a persistent record of terrorist attacks or kidnappings. The vast majority of foreign states have good records of maintaining public order and protecting residents and visitors within their borders.

Most terrorist attacks are the result of long and careful planning. Just as a car thief is attracted first to an unlocked car with the key in the ignition, terrorists are looking for undefended, easily accessible targets who follow predictable patterns. The chances of a tourist, traveling with an unpublicized itinerary, being the victim of terrorism are slight—it would amount to being at the wrong place at the wrong time. In addition, many terrorist groups, seeking publicity for political causes within their own country or region, are not specifically looking for American targets.

Nevertheless, you should take precautions. In addition to general safety practices, here are some tips that can serve as practical and psychological deterrents to would-be terrorists.

(*See Street Crime, Travel*),

When Traveling

☐ Schedule direct flights if possible. Try to minimize the time you spend in the public area of an airport, which is less protected. Move quickly from the check-in counter to the secured areas. When you reach your destination, leave the airport as quickly as possible.

☐ Avoid luggage tags, dress, and behavior that may identify you as an American. Sweatshirts and T-shirts with U.S. university logos are commonly worn throughout Europe, but leave other obvious U.S. logos or apparel at home.

☐ Keep an eye out for suspicious abandoned packages or briefcases. Report them to airport security or other authorities and leave the area promptly.

☐ Never agree to take a package with you that doesn't belong to you.

☐ Avoid obvious terrorist targets and places where American and Westerners are known to congregate.

In High-Risk Areas

If you travel in a high-risk area, the State Department advises that you do the following:

- ☐ Discuss with your family what they would do in case of an emergency, in addition to making sure your affairs are in order before leaving home.

- ☐ Register with the U.S. Embassy upon arrival. This makes it easier to locate you if someone at home needs to get in touch with you, and, more to the point, if you need to be evacuated during an emergency.

- ☐ Inform someone you know and trust what your travel plans are. Let him or her know of any changes.

- ☐ Be cautious about discussing personal matters, your itinerary, or program with anyone else.

- ☐ Don't leave any personal or business papers in your hotel room.

- ☐ Watch for people following you or "loiterers" observing your comings and goings.

- ☐ Keep a mental note of safe havens, such as police stations, hotels, and hospitals.

- ☐ Avoid predictable times and routes of travel, and report any suspicious activity to local police and the nearest U.S. Embassy or consulate.

- ☐ Select your own taxicabs at random—don't take a cab that is not clearly identified as a taxi.

- ☐ Compare the face of the driver to the one posted on his license. If they don't match, don't get in.

- ☐ Travel with others, if possible.

❏ Be sure of the identity of visitors before you open the door of your hotel room. Don't meet strangers at unknown or remote locations.

❏ Refuse unexpected packages.

❏ Formulate a plan of action for what you would do if a bomb explodes or if there is gunfire nearby.

❏ Check for loose wires or other suspicious details regarding your car.

❏ Be sure your vehicle is in good operating condition in case you need to resort to high-speed or evasive driving.

❏ Drive with the windows closed in crowded streets; bombs can be thrown through open windows.

❏ If you are ever in a situation where somebody starts shooting, drop to the floor or get down as low as possible, and don't move until you're sure the danger has passed. Do not attempt to help rescuers, and do not pick up a weapon. If possible, shield yourself behind or under a solid object. If you must move, crawl on your stomach.

In a Hostage Taking

If you are in a hostage situation, keep in mind that the most dangerous phases of most hijacking or hostage situations are the beginning and, if there is a rescue attempt, the end. At the outset, the terrorists typically are tense, and they may behave irrationally. It is vital that you remain calm and alert.

❏ Don't try to be a hero.

❏ Avoid resistance and sudden or threatening movements. Do not struggle or try to escape unless you are certain of success.

- ☐ Follow orders.

- ☐ Make a concerted effort to relax. Breathe deeply and prepare yourself mentally, physically, and emotionally for the possibility of a long ordeal.

- ☐ Try to stay inconspicuous; avoid direct eye contact, and avoid looking as if you're observing your captors' actions.

- ☐ Assume a mode of passive cooperation. Talk normally. Do not complain, avoid belligerency, and comply with all orders and instructions.

- ☐ If questioned, keep your answers short. Don't volunteer information or make unnecessary overtures.

- ☐ Keep your opinions to yourself.

- ☐ Maintain your sense of personal dignity and gradually increase your requests for personal comforts. Make these requests in a reasonable low-key manner.

- ☐ In a drawn-out situation, try to establish a rapport with your captors, avoiding political and controversial topics.

- ☐ Establish a daily program of mental and physical activity. Don't be afraid to ask for anything you need or want— medicine, books, pencils, and so forth.

- ☐ Eat what they give you, even if it doesn't look or taste appealing. A loss of appetite and weight is normal, but you must keep up your strength.

- ☐ Don't drink alcohol.

- ☐ Think positively; avoid a sense of despair. Remember that you are a valuable commodity to your captors. It is important to them to keep you alive and well.

- ☐ If you're taken hostage, pay attention to as many details as possible—the route you take, characteristics of your kidnappers, and so forth.

Other Precautions

☐ Consider a letter-bomb scanner. You can get a compact
desktop device that sounds an alarm and flashes an LED
(light-emitting diode) if it detects any metallic device in a
letter or package up to 14 inches wide and 1 inch thick.

☐ Be very calm when confronted by terrorists and speak
softly.

☐ If you're kidnapped, don't try to escape unless chances
look pretty good that you'll succeed. Odds are on your side
for being rescued or released unhurt.

☐ If you're locked in a trunk and can find something to use as
a small screwdriver, remove the small screws holding the
plastic trim over the lock mechanism. Then you can pop
open the lock with the same implement.

CONCLUSION

ACT ON YOUR ANXIETY

It makes sense to be concerned about your safety. The world is a violent place. But when you have knowledge, you have power. What we want to give you is the power to be safe.

When you know where, when, and how you're most at risk, you can act on that knowledge. Often you can avoid locations that are the sites of many crimes, such as staying out of city parks at night, or you can make changes that alter the odds in your favor—like deciding to keep your doors and windows always locked at home.

Our suggestions have ranged from the simple to the complex, from an attitude (seem confident) to an action (have your keys out as you approach your car) to suggestions on alarms and equipment. What works best in your life is for you to decide. But whatever you choose, we urge you to use it consistently. Always have a quarter tank of gas in your car. Never read a book while you wait for the bus. Always turn your alarm on as you leave your car.

The physical changes we have written about are generally one-shot deals. You change the locks in your new apartment, and that's it. You don't have to worry about doing that again. You arrange to have your social security checks deposited directly into the bank. That's it. Changes like these are relatively straightforward and easy. The ones that can be harder are those relating to how you act.

It may take some time before using these suggestions feels comfortable and automatic. You may feel silly locking your car door at the convenience store when you know you're only going to be inside for five minutes. You may think you look foolish carrying an umbrella on a clear day. You may be tired at the end of the day and not want to walk around your house before you go to bed, double-checking that the doors and windows are secure. Take comfort: the more often you incorporate these suggestions into your life, the easier they will become.

Think of our suggestions as safety belts. Many of us did not wear our car safety belts consistently before there was a big campaign to encourage it and laws were passed insisting on it. Most of us gradually learned to fasten up before we started up. Now it's an ingrained habit. We don't think twice about strapping ourselves in. In fact, it feels weird *if we don't.* Make the rest of your personal security a mind-set and a habit.

It's likely that you read the sections of this book that are of most concern to you right now. Terrific. Frankly, even if you read the whole book, what will stick with you most are the items that apply directly to your life now. Our minds sift through information we take in and hang on best to pertinent data. That's why, when you take computer training, you remember the computer commands you need for your day-to-day work and have to refer to the manual when you hit a less-frequent task, even though you know you covered it in class.

Because our minds operate this way, and because our situations change, you need to reread this book occasionally. Sometimes it will be for new information, like how to stay safe in a hotel. But it will serve you well if you read simply for a refresher course. You will benefit by going through the checklists, ticking off what you have done, and deciding what else you need to do. Use this book as a resource.

We believe that safety should be simple. That's why we have broken down our information into a clearly accessible format. We think that if it's not simple, people won't bother. And there have been plenty of burglars to attest to that when they enter a home easily and see that a sophisticated alarm system hasn't been switched on.

We have provided the facts and suggestions. The next part is up to you. You must make the changes in your life that will improve your odds of staying safe. We can't take the key out of the ignition for you when you park. We can't keep your children from going out after dark. But you can.

Obviously you don't need to do *everything* in this book. Decide which you need to do, and do them. Knowledge and common sense will see you through almost everything. We have given you knowledge about crime and protective measures. We urge you to use this knowledge and to exercise your common sense. Prudence pays off.

We can't guarantee that you will be safe. You have taken an important first step, however, by reading this book. By doing so, you show that you're concerned about personal safety. Recognizing that crime can happen to you means that you can go to the next steps: taking precautions and being prepared. Being able to act on your anxieties will bring you self-confidence and peace of mind. You, not the criminal, will control your life. Not frozen by fears, you will act prudently and still be able to do what you want.

INDEX

YOUR COMMENTS

A great deal of effort has been taken to make this book as comprehensive as possible. Your input is welcome; it will help make future editions more complete and timely. Please send your comments and suggestions to Attn.: Crime, Brassey's (US), Editorial Office, 8000 Westpark Drive, First Floor, McLean, VA 22102.

ABOUT THE AUTHORS

James B. Motley, Ph.D., is an internationally known and widely published author, lecturer, and consultant to the U.S. government and the private sector. He has been the vice president for a major security firm, directed research on security policy and planning and crisis management for a number of U.S. organizations, and appeared before the White House Task Force on Combating Terrorism.

Lois M. Baron is a professional journalist. Her writing has appeared in such publications as *Psychology Today, The Journal of Defense & Diplomacy,* and *The Washington Post.* She has done work for *U.S. News & World Report, Europe* magazine, and the World Bank, among other business and publication clients.

ABOUT THE AUTHORS